JONESING

This book is dedicated to the

memory of Claiborne Joiner, Jr.

My friend. My brother.

We miss you and we love you.

*The good die young…but the real live
forever.*

Rest easy.

Chapter One

"His dick little…"

"**K**ERRINGTON!!! You did not sleep with that man?!?!?!" Kerrington chuckles to herself and replies to the text. "Girl, naw. How could I? I just told you his dick lil." Lindsey looks at the phone puzzled and starts to text feverishly. "Kerry, how do you know that man's meat is little if y'all didn't have sex?" "Girl, he came to the office to bring me lunch in these grey sweatpants. Them sweatpants were not sweatpantsing! It was giving kibbles & bits," Kerrington texts back. Shae immediately

Chapter One

chimes in defense of Kerrington. "Exactly!! You ain't gotta sleep with a man to know if he packin' or not. A man will lie ALL DAY LONG, but them grey sweatpants will tell the truth and nothing but the truth, Your Honor!"

Welcome to the female text thread. Where the only lie that's told is how a woman truly feels about a man. In this text thread, aptly named *"The Delta Divas"*, three friends from Dallas, Tx, Kerrington Janel Jones, Lindsey Rayfield, and Shae Dixon, share everything, sometimes too much. They went to the same high school, pledged Delta Sigma Theta together (hence the group text name), and graduated from Prairie View A&M University. They've cried together, they've laughed together, and they've been arrested together (if you haven't been to the Bayou Classic and gotten arrested, have you *really* been to

Chapter One

the Bayou Classic??). There is nothing these ladies haven't seen and there isn't anything they wouldn't do for each other.

"Kerry, don't you think it's a little shallow to ghost a nigga just because of a dick print?" Lindsey asks. "Uh…judgement! And correction, you mean lack of a dick print," Kerrington shoots back. She then quickly followed with another text. "And Lindsey didn't you stop talking to L.C. when you found out the L stood for Leroy??" "Uh uh, wait, that was different." Lindsey texts. "He was talking about naming his son after him. How the fuck I look yelling 'C'mere Lil Leroy, let me tie your shoe? Bitch! Lie!" She fires back. Shae sends three laughing emojis as the exchange between Kerrington and Lindsey clearly entertains her. "You hoes crazy!! We all are shallow, but KJ, you are water-in-a-stand-up-shower shallow." Shae texts.

"Okay, so what you hoes not finna do is gang up on me this morning. And Shae, you thought you ate! EVERYONE is shallow, some just more than others," Kerrington fires back. "But I agree, I have been known to be a bit more shallow than others. But I like what I like, and if I'm going to be dealing with a man, I think he should be everything I want him to be. I mean, after all, why settle?" Kerrington asks. "Kerry, you're right; no one should settle. But being picky in an effort to get exactly what you want and hiding behind it in an effort to protect yourself ain't the same thing," Lindsey adds. Shae texts a GIF of a hooded Beyonce' sipping from a straw and turns around as if to say *"checkmate."* "That part," she added. Kerrington quickly texts back, "Girl, ain't

Chapter One

nobody hiding behind nothing. Now can a bitch take her morning shit in peace??" Kerrington slams her phone on the bathroom sink counter and stands there for a few seconds in silence, staring aimlessly at a corner of the floor. "Fat head bitch always think she right. Uglass." Kerrington grimes. As she exits the bathroom, she hears her phone ding to alert her of a text message. She picks it up and opens the phone. "I know you just called me a bitch," Lindsey texts. "But ya daddy told me ya momma one, too. Love you! Smooches!" Kerrington bursts out in laughter. Lindsey always knew how to make her laugh, even when she didn't want to. She always told her what she needed to hear and not what she wanted to hear.

Kerrington sat on the edge of her king-sized bed and thought about what her best friend had just

Chapter One

said. Was she really hiding behind her high standards in order to protect herself or more importantly, her heart? She'd been hurt before and wasn't too interested in experiencing that type of pain again. "So, what if I'm guarded?" she pondered to herself out loud. "Who's going to look out for me better than myself??"

Kerrington Janel Jones is a 5'4 165lbs mortgage loan officer. She wears her weight well, as much of it is stored in her hips, ass, and thighs. She consistently gets compliments on her pillowy soft, smooth caramel skin complexion, and most women pay to get the eyelashes she was born with. Her taper fade is always fresh, crisp, and wavy. She frequents the barbershop weekly to ensure her hair never looks out of place.

Chapter One

Her deep trance is interrupted by the ringing of her phone. It's Shae. Kerrington pauses for a moment and then answers, "What, bitch?" "Ewww, that attitude sho ain't it. But I'll let you make it since Lindsey did just serve you," Shae replied. "Lindsey ain't serve a damn thang this way! I just be letting her think that sometimes," Kerrington responds. "Letting her?? Oh, you mean by going to take a shit??" Shae replies while laughing. "Girl, you are a piece of work, hunny!" Shae continued. Annoyed, Kerrington shot back, "Sooo, you called for what reason, again?" she asked. "Bitch, I called to tell you that it's okay to heal. And in her own way, that's all Lindsey is trying to tell you,too." Shae said.

Kerrington knew her friends meant well and were just trying to offer their support as they normally do. "I know, Shae. I just get a little bent

Chapter One

outta shape when I'm reminded about my current situation and how I got here. She was right; I just didn't wanna hear it," Kerrington said.

"I know, friend, but you really have to give dating a chance. Heal first, then HONESTLY put yourself back out there and not just a part of you," Shae replied. "You're right. Both of you are. But I really don't think healing is the issue. It's the putting myself back out there that has me worried," Kerrington said. "Well, friend…if you're still worried about putting yourself back on the market, then you're not done healing," Shae said. There was a pause on the phone for a few seconds. "Wow. I never looked at it like that," Kerrington said. "Friend, where are you getting all this new-found wisdom from??" "Ha," Shae said with a laugh. "You tried it.

Chapter One

But I've been reading this book about dating, and clearly, yo ass need to read it, too," she said. "Shae? Reading?? Damn, bitch, it must be some pictures in there!" Kerrington jokes. "Uhm, while you're laughing, it's something edible on the cover chile…whew. But I'm reading a chapter in that book that talks about people exactly like you!" Kerrington scoffs. "People like me?? And what in the hell is that supposed to mean??" Shae laughs. "People who aren't being honest with themselves. People like *YOU*," she shot back. "Okay, hold on. What's the name of this book?" Kerrington asks.

"So, You Say You Wanna Start Dating? We just started reading it in my book club. And hunny, this man is dropping some gems, you hear me?? I really didn't think I wanted to hear anything about dating from a man, but this book is so insightful. I'm

Chapter One

telling you, KJ; there is an entire chapter where he's talking directly to you!" Shae excitedly claims. With her interest clearly peaked, Kerrington is ready to see what this book has to offer. "Okay, okay…you and ya lil book club do be putting me on some good literature, so I guess I'll check it out." "Girl, say less." Shae replied. "I can get an extra copy from the club. I'll meet you at the shop Friday and give it to you."

Shae, Kerrington, and Lindsey went to the same place to get their hair done. It was a barbershop that also doubled as a salon in the back. They all went every Friday after work. "Okay, Shae, that sounds good. This little fella better not be on no Kevin Samuels shit either." Kerrington quipped. "Ugh… no, ma'am. Why do you think I'd even read some smut like that?? Yuck." Shae responds. "Oh, ok. Girl,

Chapter One

I'm just checking. Well, let me get back to my morning. I gotta get to the office and handle some things I didn't finish up yesterday."

Kerrington said. "Alrighty, bestie. And don't forget to release that demon you were lying about earlier." Shae said while laughing loudly. "Ugh! Bye, bitch!" Kerrington yelled.

Kerrington knew she needed to get herself together if she was ever going to put herself back on the market officially. She knew deep down that it wasn't fair to lead men on if she knew she truly had no intentions of being serious with them. Her last relationship almost scarred her beyond repair, and she knew she owed it to herself to truly heal and try to become the finished product that she knew she could be.

Chapter One

Kerrington's last relationship ended in heartbreak. Her first and only time ever being in love was with a married but separated man. His wife, unknowingly, solicited the services of the best mortgage loan officer in the city. She said that her and her husband wanted to start over fresh and what better way to start than in a new house. Imagine Kerrington's surprise when she saw the love of her life pull up with his wife to see the brand-new house she picked out for them. The word hurt would be an understatement. She was devastated. As difficult as it was, she pushed through with the sale without making a scene. Smiling on the outside, all while crying on the inside. She proceeded to block his phone calls and text messages. She blocked him on all social media sites. She ignored his pleads outside her front door for days. As his attempts to reach out

Chapter One

started to wane, a mysterious package appeared at his home. Its contents consisted of screenshots of text messages between him and another woman. Explicit photos of him performing lewd acts on a woman whose face had been distorted.

Hell hath no fury like a woman scorned.

Afterward, Kerrington went through the motions that heartbreak can bring. She wasn't as active as she was before. She began to shun her family and friends. She began wearing dark-coloured clothes and nail polishes, which seemed to be tied to her moods. She, ultimately, just wasn't herself. Once she began to get back in the groove of things, she swore that she would never become *"that"* girl again. And she has been hell-bent on keeping that promise ever since.

Chapter One

The morning was getting away from Kerrington, so she started to prepare herself for the day. She took a quick shower, brushed her teeth, and rubbed lotion all over her body. She put on a black & white, geometric print, long-sleeved pencil dress. She sat on the bed and put on some black suede heels that were strapped at the ankles. She then put on some earrings and accessories, removed her scarf to make sure each and every hair was in place, grabbed her Louis Vuitton purse and was out the door.

Chapter Two

"…because you are fuckin crazy!!!"

"I'm crazy because I love yo stupid ass??"

"NOO!!!" Joaquin yelled. "You're crazy because you drove all the way to the barbershop just because I didn't answer your calls!"

"And?? Da fuck?? You damn right I did!" LeSean shouts while shaking her neck and getting on her toes to get as close to Joaquin's face as she can. "You been ignoring my calls and my texts like I won't pull up on yo ass!" LeSean continued. "That's the point,

LeSean. We're not together!! I don't have to answer ANY of your calls or respond to any of your text messages!!" Joaquin replied aggressively. "Come to think of it, how in the hell did you know I was at the shop anyway?? Yo crazy ass was just riding around till you found me??" Joaquin asked. "Nigga, don't worry 'bout how I found you. I knew you was up here with ya lil' dusty ass friends like you always are. You pay more attention to them than you do me!!" LeSean fires off.

Joaquin Rylan Stevenson, a 29-year-old personal trainer, had been dating LeSean Everett, a 26-year-old 911 dispatcher, for a few months, off and on, until they decided to give a relationship a try and fully commit to one another. That *"relationship"* was over before it even started. There was rarely a moment where they weren't arguing, fussing at one

Chapter Two

another, or fighting about something petty. Their relationship was everything you'd think a toxic relationship would consist of. Each time Joaquin has tried to end the relationship, LeSean promises to change her toxic ways, only to revert back to who she truly is and sends them both back to square one.

"I come here to get peace and get away from yo throwed off ass. LeSean, I can't do this anymore. You are fuckin crazy!!" Joaquin yells. "Peace?!?!" LeSean quipped. "You go to Groove and VonEric for peace?? Two niggas, Joaquin??" Joaquin stops her before she can say another word. "Say, man...you know damn well what I mean. I come to the shop to kick it, hang out, and just chill. Stop with the funny shit, LeSean." Joaquin explained. "All we do is fuck and fight. That shit is getting old. You going through my phone and calling random numbers. You always questioning me. Poppin' up at my studio. You pick fights about the pettiest shit. I'm just sick of it! You are bat-shit crazy!" Joaquin yells. "Whatever, nigga. I'ma show yo ass what crazy REALLY looks like. Keep ignoring my calls! I'ma show you. I promise you dat!" LeSean fires back.

LeSean got in her white Lexus coup and drove off, fishtailing as she went around the corner. Joaquin, clearly frustrated, walked back into the barbershop only to be greeted by the laughs and jokes of his friends. "Hey, Day-Day, dat crazy bitch out there again!" Groove shouted as the barbershop erupted in laughter, mocking Uncle Elroy from *Next Friday*. "Man, fuck y'all." Joaquin said while grabbing a seat. "Wah (Wah is what they called him instead of Joaquin), you can't be letting her come to my fine establishment scaring off my patrons."

Chapter Two

VonEric pleaded." "Fine establishment?!?" Groove said with a chuckle. "Cap! Nigga, it's a giant roach in the restroom handing out napkins after we wash our hands." He said while still laughing. "Straight up. And it looks like you running numbers and selling moonshine in the back." Joaquin added.

"Man, fuck y'all. I got the hottest barbershop & salon in the city." VonEric said defensively. "Nigga, the only thing that's hot in here is these clippers that's on my damn head. They not gonna explode mid-cut again, are they??" Groove asked.

Joaquin, Groove, and VonEric have been best friends since high school. They all lettered in football and basketball. They attended Texas Southern University together and have been virtually inseparable since they were teenagers. The best of friends. They even went and had John 15:13 tattooed on the inside of their right forearms as a sign of loyalty, brotherhood, love, and respect for one another. They all went on to become business owners after college. They pooled their resources and bought commercial properties. Groove is the DJ and owner of the hottest night spot in the city. VonEric is the owner of a barbershop/salon in downtown Dallas. And Joaquin has his own fitness studio and has sculpted some of the best-looking bodies in the area.

"Man, shut up and sit still," VonEric told Groove. "But, Wah, be real…that thang hot, ain't it??" Groove asked with all the interest in the world. Joaquin looks at Groove puzzled. "Nigga, what?" he asked. "Dat monkey! I know dat thang hot! They say the crazy ones have the best sex." Groove explained. "Dat mouth gotta be hot, too. No way in hell this nigga just sticking around cause the box good." VonEric adds. Joaquin sat there for a second, staring aimlessly at the floor, and then a smirk slowly appeared on his face. As if he was having a flashback. "Say, bruh…LeSean is the TRUTH…and a half!!" Joaquin proclaimed. "I knew it!! I fuckin' knew it!!" Groove shouts excitingly. But Joaquin laughter fades suddenly.

"But that's just it. That's really all it was. Sex. I mean, she has some other good qualities, but, man, as you get older, you gotta be more than just fine or just have good sex. That shit gets old after a while." Joaquin stated. "Preach, young boy. Pass the got damn collection plate around." VonEric yelled. "You spittin' now, bruh," he continued. "Fa real, man. Eventually, you want someone you can build with, and most importantly, find peace in and add to their happiness. LeSean just ain't that woman…at least not for me." Joaquin stated. "That's real, bruh. I feel you on that. The single life is cool and all, but sometimes you wanna meet that one, ya know?" Groove stated. "Damn, Groove. I ain't never heard you speak like this. Where is all this coming from??" Joaquin asked eagerly. "I'm just redirecting my focus when it comes to dating. I'm tired of dating for sport. I wanna start dating with a purpose. I been reading this book, and…" Groove is immediately interrupted by Joaquin and VonEric. "Nigga you been doing what??" they asked simultaneously. "Man, chill on me. I been reading this book called *So You Say You Wanna Start Dating*'. It's really changed my outlook on dating." Groove explained. "Man, I don't know what's more unbelievable: yo ass been reading or you starting to take dating seriously," VonEric said

Chapter Two

with a laugh. "Yeeeaaaa, I'ma take the reading," Joaquin said. "In case you cornball ass niggas forgot, I graduated with a higher GPA than both of you clowns," Groove said, emphatically. "Fool, that's because you were fucking your tutor, and she was doing all of your work." Joaquin shoots back. "Which clearly means I'm smarter than BOTH of y'all. Y'all were working harder, and I was working smarter. Maybe you two shoulda been doing what I was doing." Groove said in defense of himself.

"Boy. Shut up. Where can I find this book at? If you're reading it, I most definitely need to take a look at it." Joaquin asks. "I'm almost done, bro. You can get my copy." Groove said. "That's a bet. Well, I'm finna slide, fellas. Got an appointment with a new client at the studio in a few." Joaquin said while grabbing his belongings. "Cool, you coming by The

Chapter Two

Spot tonight? It's Lady's Night." Groove asks. "Fa sho, you picking me up, Von?" Joaquin asked. "Bet dat. I'll be there at 10:30. And don't wear one of them shirts that show your nipples. You can't ride with me dressed like that." VonEric said. "The ladies love a lil' chest. Take note, young buck," Joaquin said as he was motioning towards the door.

As the door opened, the prettiest, caramel-skinned, big, bright-eyed, sexiest female Joaquin had ever laid eyes on walked through the door. He was stunned but quickly caught himself before the moment became awkward. "I'm sorry, excuse me," Joaquin said as he held the door open for her from the inside. "Oh, no, I'm sorry. Excuse me," the beautiful lady said as she looked up from her phone and locked eyes with the most attractive, most

Chapter Two

handsome, chocolate, full-bearded, 6-foot-1-inch man she had ever seen in her life.

Kerrington paused for a split second in admiration of what she was looking at and then quickly got herself together before her lustful eyes became too noticeable. She sat and waited for her turn to get in the barber's chair to get her edge tighten. Still mesmerized by what she had just laid eyes on, she didn't hear VonEric speaking to her. "KJ, you ready?" VonEric asked. She answered as she shook out of her daze. "Yea, Von, I'm ready." She replied. "You ready for me?" she asked. "Yep, I'm almost done with Groove." VonEric said. "Oh, hey, Groove, I didn't even see you sitting there". Kerrington said while still a tab bit astonished. "Sounds like a short joke, but I'll let it slide if you come by The Spot tonight. It's Ladies Night!"

Chapter Two

Groove said. Kerrington laughed. "Boy, ain't nobody laughing at your height, but let me ask my girls if they wanna come to your lil' club tonight," she said, "You said 'lil'. That's cute. But I'll see y'all there. Stop acting like any one of y'all turning down free liquor. Be there before 12." Groove said as he paid VonEric and exited the shop.

"Groove is so silly. Hey, have you seen Shae come through here today?" Kerrington asked VonEric. "Naw, not today. Why? What's up?" he asked. "Oh, nothing. I was just trying to catch her in here before I leave; she has a book she said she was going to give me." Kerrington replied. "Oh yea, what's it about?" VonEric asked. "Something about dating. She mentioned it this morning. So, I said I would check it out." "That's wild. Groove was just in here talking about a dating book. Is it called, *So*

Chapter Two

You Say You Wanna Start Dating?" VonEric asked.

"Yes!! That's it!! Wait…Groove is reading a book??

Oh, I definitely gotta check this out." Kerrington said

as VonEric laughed loudly. "Man, I said the same

thing!!"

As VonEric starts to shape up Kerrington's

hair, Shae walks in. "Hey, bestie. Hey, Vonny." Shae

says as she speaks to everyone. "Hey, girl. I was just

asking about you. Did you bring the book?"

Kerrington asked. "I sure did. Here ya go." Shae said.

"Thank you! Hey, you and Lindsey wanna go to The

Spot tonight?" Kerrington asked. "Bitch, you know

it's two things I'm always ready to do: get fine and

get drunk," Shae replied. Kerrington laughs

uncontrollably. "Not you being an alcoholic. I'll call

Lindsey when I get outta this chair and let her know."

Chapter Two

Kerrington finished getting her haircut and called

Lindsey to let her know about tonight's festivities.

Chapter Three

"Giiiiirl, my mouth got watery." Kerrington said.
"You was ready to risk it all??" Lindsey asked.

"And WAS!!!"

Kerrington, Shae, and Lindsey sat at the bar inside The Spot and discussed Kerrington's run-in with Joaquin earlier at the barbershop. "And he smelled so damn good! Girl, everything about that man was perfect! His haircut, his beard. Bitch, his eyebrows were even shaped perfectly." Kerrington said as they all laughed. "But who is he? What's his name?" Shae yelled while trying to talk over the music. "That's the thing!" Kerrington replied. "I don't know. I've never seen him at the shop before." "You didn't ask VonEric who he was?" Shae asked. "Girl, naw. I don't need him going back and telling nobody I asked about them. These niggas talk too much." Kerrington said. "But Kerry, how are you in here lusting over this man like this and don't even know who he is and didn't even try to find out??" Linsdey asks inquisitively. "Lindsey, I don't know. But I have literally been thinking about that man ever since I saw him. My goodness. That man was so damn FINE!" Kerrington replied.

"Kerrington Jones?? How long has she been coming to the shop??" Joaquin asked. "Man, for about a year and a half, I think," VonEric answered.

Chapter Three

"Bruh, she been coming to the shop all this time, and I ain't never seen her??" Joaquin pondered. "Well, you come on Saturdays. She comes on Friday's when she leaves the office. She's a mortgage loan officer. Probably the best in the city." VonEric explained. "That's it!!" Joaquin shouted. I've seen her face on a few billboards in the city. I thought I seen her somewhere."

"Fella's! Glad y'all made it. It's tough in here tonight!" Groove said as he walked up and joined the conversation. "You ain't lied yet," VonEric added. "What's up with this fool? Wah! What's up, man? You good??" Groove asked with a lot of concern. "Man, he trippin' over Kerrington. He saw her at the shop today." VonEric said. 'Kerrington Jones?? She bad. I'm talking B-A-D-D badd! She is supposed to be in here tonight. Her and her homegirls." Groove said. "Daaaaamn, that's right. You did ask her at the shop, huh?" VonEric asked. "In here? Tonight??" Joaquin asked. "Yes, sir, I asked her before I left the shop," Groove replied. "Bet! I gotta find her. Tonight! And the moment I do, you better play something slow, too." Joaquin said excitingly. "Damn, nigga. You trying to holla at her or strip for her? Boy, you aint got no motion like that." Groove said while VonEric laughed. "Nigga, just do it. You got a bird's eye view from up there in the DJ booth anyway. You should see her before all of us." Joaquin stated. "Bruh, chill. You my nigga. I got you!" Groove said calmly. "My man! Let's get off this bar and see what we can find," said Joaquin. The guys split up in hopes of finding Kerrington. And no sooner than they grab their drinks and walk away

Chapter Three

from the bar, Joaquin is confronted by none other than LeSean.

"See, KJ, that's why you need to read that book I gave you. There is an entire chapter on shooting your shot." Shae said. "You over here worried about what Von might say when that should really be the least of your concerns." "Shae, you're right." Kerrington said." "But I don't like people in my business. And I can speak for myself. I don't need VonEric black ass speaking

for me." Lindsey chimed in. "You right, friend. But you also just said Shae was right. And I see both points, but you did say you had been thinking about him since you saw him. Sounds like you need to make a move, friend." Lindsey added. "Yea, but I ain't trying to seem thirsty either." Kerrington said.

Chapter Three

"Bitch, that thirsty shit is played," Shae said. "Nothing and no one, not even you hoes, would stand in between me and something I want." And just as Kerrington was about to respond, she felt someone gently grab her by the waist. Startled, she quickly turns around, and she's shocked by who she sees. "Kerrington Jones. Damn. A nigga brings you lunch, and you straight ghost him." The tall, light-skinned gentlemen said. "Korey!" Kerrington said, still in shock. "Hey…"

"At this point, this is stalking. What the fuck, LeSean?!" Joaquin said, clearly frustrated. "All I wanna do is talk, Joaquin, but you got yo trifling ass in here being a slut!" said LeSean. "LeSean, I am literally just standing here having a drink with my niggas. What is wrong with you??" Joaquin asked. "You are what's wrong with me," LeSean shot back.

Chapter Three

"I just wanna talk to you!" "Ok, LeSean, we can talk. Just not in here." Joaquin said. "Where then, Joaquin?" she asked. "Go to your car. Let me finish this drink, and I'll be out there in a minute." Joaquin said. "I promise." "Joaquin, please don't play with me. We really need to talk." LeSean said, anxiously. "I got you," he replied. "I'ma finish this drink, and I'll be out there."

LeSean walks away, and Joaquin takes a sigh of relief. "Wah, I know damn well you not going out there to talk to that girl??" VonEric asked. "Hell naw!!" Joaquin replied. "I just had to

get her outta here so I can find Kerrington." "Quick on ya feet, young boy. I taught you well." Groove stated. "Fa sho, now let's move around." Joaquin ordered.

Chapter Three

As they maneuver through the club for almost an hour, they finally find who they were looking for. "Say, Wah, there she is, right there!!" VonEric said as he pointed her out. "That damn sure is her!! But who in the hell let Boris Kodjoe in this bitch?" Joaquin said as he looked on, puzzled. "I don't know, but it looks like he knows Kerrington pretty damn good. They close as fuck!" VonEric answered. "BRUH!! I fuckin' knew it!! Ain't no woman looking like THAT gonna be single." Joaquin said dejectedly. "Oh, well. It was what it was. I'ma finish this drink, and I'ma slide." Joaquin said. "Nigga, that's your fourth drink. You need to slow down. You know you're a lightweight! And besides, we ain't even been in here that long. You gonna let her ruin your night?" VonEric asked. Joaquin paused for a moment and then answered. "Yes". "But you rode

Chapter Three

with me." VonEric replied. "Uber," an annoyed Joaquin said as he was still looking in Kerrington's direction.

"How you been, beautiful?" Korey asked. "Uh...I'm ok", Kerrington replied. "Y'all, this is Korey. Korey, these are my best friends, Shae and Lindsey." Kerrington said as she introduced everyone. "Evening, ladies. Hope I'm not interrupting." Korey said. Lindsey leaned in and whispered to Kerrington. "Bitch, who is this??" Kerrington whispered back, "Korey!" Lindsey stood there confused. "Kibbles & Bits" Kerrington whispered again. "Oooooooh. Ouh." Lindsey replied as her facial expression quickly changed from curious to disappointment. She then turns around and fills Shae in on who the mystery man really is. As

Chapter Three

Korey continued to talk, Kerrington sent the distress signal to get her out of this predicament.

"Kerrington, are you ready to go yet? We gotta get on the road pretty early tomorrow." Lindsey asked loud enough so they both could hear her. "Ouh, you right. We need to go. I'm sorry, Korey, but I really gotta go. I'm driving to New Orleans in the morning, so I better get home and get some rest." Kerrington advised. "Oh, ok. Cool. Be careful. Will I hear from you tomorrow?" Korey asked. "No," Kerrington said without thinking. "Huh?" Korey replied. "No doubt!!" Kerrington responded as they hugged.

The girls quickly usher Kerrington out of the club. "Bitch, did you just tell that man no doubt? What in the 1995 was that?" Shae asked. "Ugh, girl, I don't know. When he asked if he was gonna hear from me tomorrow, I said no so damn fast, I had to think of something to clean it up." Kerrington responded. As she pulls her keys from her purse, she stops. "IT'S HIM!!"

Joaquin walks outside only to see LeSean waiting in the front of the parking lot. "What's up, LeSean? Joaquin asked as he got in her car. "When are you going to stop acting like this, Joaquin? You know you miss me." LeSean said as she leaned over to kiss and hug him. "You really think I miss crazy?" Joaquin asked, as he slowly backed away. "You said you wanted to talk. You got me fucked up if you I'm this stupid." Joaquin continued. "Nigga, this ain't about yo stupid ass being stupid. You been drinking, and we both know how you get when liquor is in your system. Stop playing and give this dick." LeSean says as she reaches for his crotch.

Chapter Three

"But why is he getting in the passenger side?" Lindsey asked. "Cause the driver is finna go to work on him, girl, look!" Shae says as they all look attentively through the vehicle's back window as the two silhouettes get closer." "Shoulda known ain't NO man THAT fine is single." Kerrington stated. "Or a hoe." Shae added. "Or a hoe." Lindsey repeated. Kerrington let out a

deep sigh. "Let's go before Korey brings his worrisome ass out here." She stated. "Ouh, girl, yes!! I think he got a nipple ring, too." Shae responded.

They piled in Kerrington's black BMW X6 and drove off. As Lindsey and Shae continued to talk about the night's events, Kerrington couldn't help but feel disappointed. It wasn't often she found herself excited about a man. And even though she knew absolutely nothing about the man from the

Chapter Three

barbershop, it was just fun and exciting to be that intrigued by someone, even if it were only for a few hours. She thought to herself, will this cycle ever end? The high of potentially meeting someone new and interesting, only to be let down because that's just what men do…let you down.

She gathered herself and dived into the conversation her friends were having, but she couldn't help but think, was she becoming desperate? It was really unlike her to be so off balance about a man the way she was about seeing Joaquin. She kept thinking about how she felt when she saw him get in the car and the female figure lean towards him. Why did she feel so empty over guy a guy she had never really even met?

Chapter Four

Joaquin awakes from a drunken slumber and tries to figure out where he is. "Damn, I've been asleep all this time? Fuck!" he says as he rolls over to check the time on his phone. "Yes, pumpkin head. You had a REALLY long night." LeSean said with a devilish smile on her face. "Da hell is that supposed to mean?" Joaquin asked as he turned his attention from his phone to LeSean. "Joaquin, don't play stupid. You know damn well what that means. You know how you get when you get alcohol in your system." LeSean responded with a smirk.

Joaquin paused and thought to himself for a moment. "Nah, you trippin'. I get sleepy when I get

Chapter Four

alcohol in me. So, I know ain't nothing happen last night." LeSean laughs loudly. "Honey, you didn't get sleepy until this pussy drained you. You think you're waking up this late because you were drunk??" LeSean asked as she laughed loudly again. Joaquin pauses again and looks under the sheets to find himself underwear-less. "Fuck." He says under his breath as he grabs his phone again. "Say, man...that's rape. You drugged me or something. I don't remember shit." LeSean quickly fires back. "Joaquin Stevenson, be fuckin for real. Look at me. Does it look like I would have to rape anybody?" Joaquin sat up in the bed, gazing at LeSean for a second and couldn't help but admit to himself she had a point.

Her caramel skin was flawless and glowing, just as it always did. He tried not to get lost in her

Chapter Four

deep, big brown eyes, but he couldn't help himself. Her full lips were glossy, and she had breasts the size of Australia. Even in a headscarf, LeSean looked radiant. Something he always admired about her. Joaquin quickly snaps out of his sunken place and orders an Uber. "Listen, I don't remember shit. So didn't shit happen? And I feel an argument brewing seeing as how we

haven't had one in the last 10 minutes. You enjoy the rest of your weekend, and I'll do the same. Good day." Joaquin said as he was getting dressed and grabbed his things.

Kerrington sat in her bed glued to the book she borrowed from Shae. She absorbed each word and intently turned each page.

Chapter Four

"Remember, anyone can shoot, but not everyone makes 'em.

What are you doing to make sure you don't miss?

I mean…we could only be talking about the rest of your life here.

The rest of your life. Kerrington found herself stuck on that last line in that chapter. She wasn't getting any younger, and she knew she was in the prime of her life. Reading that book made her want to take control of her destiny and leave the waiting for someone else. As she continued to read, she continued to think about Joaquin, and she could not get the image of him getting into that car with another woman out of her head.

She was snatched away from her trance by the ringing of her phone. It was a facetime call from

Chapter Four

Lindsey. "Hey, Lindsey." She answered. "Ouh, you don't have to look so excited," Lindsey responded. "Oh, girl, I'm sorry. I just been reading this book Shae gave me. What's up?" Kerrington said. "Me and Shae are going to brunch downtown. Put some clothes on and take some of that ugly off. We'll be there in an hour." Lindsey advised. "Awww, that sounds fun, but I'ma stay in today, bestie. I'm still tired from last night." Kerrington said. "Uh uh. No, ma'am. My friend don't turn down no mimosa's. What's going on, Kerry?" Lindsey asked.

Kerrington sat back against her plush, suede headboard and removed her glasses. "Lindsey, I just cannot seem to get that guy out of my mind?" She stated. "Who? Shemar Moore from last night??" Lindsey asked. "Oh, girl, hell no! The guy from the barbershop. The one from the club last night."

Chapter Four

Kerrington answered. She continued to confide in Lindsey. "Girl, I know I sound crazy, but when we locked eyes at the barbershop, I felt something jolt through my body that I hadn't felt before. It only lasted a second, but it felt like I'd been looking into those eyes forever.

Lindsey looked her friend in the eye and spoke some clarity about what she was feeling. "Friend, you felt a connection. That man looked you in the eyes and introduced himself to you without saying a word. Bestie, what you're feeling is intrigue. And there is nothing crazy about that." Lindsey spoke of everything that Kerrington was feeling but couldn't figure out. It made even more sense when she thought about how she had felt the night before. "Bestie, you are so right. Looking him in his eyes just felt...right." Kerrington responded. "Well, now that you know what you're feeling, what's next?" Lindsey asked. Kerrington looked down at the book she was reading and thought for a second. "I shoot my shot."

The work week breezed by for Kerrington. She constantly thought of Joaquin. She hadn't been so excited about someone since the married ex-boyfriend. And she couldn't believe it was about a man whose name she didn't even know. She tried convincing herself that seeing him get into the car with another woman meant nothing until she knew for certain that he wasn't available, but doubt would creep in. Was she getting excited about nothing? Or was she just setting herself up for a letdown from a someone whom she knew absolutely nothing about? She knew she could find out what she needed at the barbershop. She couldn't wait for Friday to get here. This was her opportunity to find out all she needed to know.

"Ms. Jones, always on time. I like that in my customers." VonEric said as he greeted Kerrington as she walked through the door. "Hey, Von. How are you today?" "I'm good...same thing?" he asked as he wrapped the barber cape around her neck. "You know it," Kerrington replied. Even though she had all week to think about it, she still had no clue on how she would ask VonEric about Joaquin without sounding interested or turning on his suspicion. As she stumbled over ideas in her head, Shae walked through the door. "Hey, bestie. Hey, Von." Shae said. "Hey, boo. You look nice." Kerrington replied.

Tossing her hair back over her shoulder, Shae replied, "I know. So, VonEric…I need to ask you about one of your customers." "Which one?" VonEric replied. "I don't know," Shae said. Never looking up from focusing on Kerrington's head, VonEric replied, "You wore a helmet in school, huh? You only had about 4 kids in your classroom." Kerrington burst out laughing as Shae gave VonEric a very piercing look. "Yo super ugly ass makes me sick. He was in here last Friday, right before I got here. Dark-skinned, wavy haircut, beard. Kinda tall." Shae said. VonEric stopped cutting and thought for a minute. "Joaquin??" he said while still guessing. "I don't know, nigga. That's why I'm asking you." Shae said sarcastically. VonEric whipped out his cell phone and went straight to Instagram. "Him?" he asked as he showed Shae his IG page. "Yep!! That's

Chapter Four

his fine ass." Shae answered. "Man, that's like my brother! What you wanna know about him for?" VonEric asked. Shae responded quickly. "I don't wanna know about him. Kerry does." Kerrington looked at Shae in shock and total disbelief that Shae outed her. Shae grabbed

her purse and looked at Kerrington with a smirk. "Laugh now, bitch." Shae said as she walked back towards the salon area.

VonEric spins Kerrington around, so they are facing one another. "KJ!! You feeling my boy??" Kerrington, clearly embarrassed, answers, "Ugh…I was until I saw him get in the car with some girl last Friday." VonEric doubles over in laughter as he leans up against his counter. Kerrington sits there confused and hits VonEric. "Von, what the hell are you laughing at? That ain't funny!" VonEric gathers himself and tries to explain. "Whew, this is too funny. Listen, he was at the club looking for YOU!"

A look of disbelief comes across Kerrington's face. "ME?!" she asked. "Yes. YOU. He had been talking about you all night. Groove told him that you and your girls were gonna be there, so we all split up looking for you. He saw you talking to some 1990's, light-skinned brother with good hair and left." VonEric replied. "Oh, no!" Kerrington said with a gasp. "You're talking about Korey. He just popped up out of nowhere. UGH, he's so fucking annoying." Then VonEric responded, "Buddie didn't look annoying that night. Y'all looked like a real couple. No cap." "No," Kerrington replied. "What you all saw was me being nice. We left just so I could get away from his fuddy duddy ass."

Then Kerrington paused. "Wait…if you're telling me he was in there looking for me, he must've found something he really liked. Because some girl was all over him in a car outside the club." Kerrington stated. VonEric quickly cut her off. "Man, that's his ex-girlfriend, LeSean. That broad is crazy. She walked up on us just as we started looking for you. He had to tell her to

go wait in the car just so he could move around and look for you. So, what YOU saw was him being nice, as well."

Kerrington felt a mixed bag of emotions at that point. Excited. Happy. Relieved. Anxious. This worked out better than she could have imagined. All of the questions she had were now finally starting to get answered. She had a name. She had a relationship status. And she even discovered that he is just as interested in her as she is in him. Now all she needed was him. VonEric was geeked. "My boy is gon' be stupid excited when I tell him about this". Then Kerrington cut him off. "No, he won't cause you ain't telling him shit." VonEric, confused, asked why. "Well, if I don't tell him, how in the hell is he going to find out, KJ??"

Kerrington thought for a second about the book. She thought about the last few lines in chapter three that had her stuck.

"Remember, anyone can shoot, but not everyone makes 'em.

What are you doing to make sure you don't miss?

I mean…we could only be talking about the rest of your life here.

Chapter Four

She had her target in sight, but she couldn't leave anything up to fate. She had to take her shot and make sure she didn't miss.

"How much are his haircuts?" Kerrington asked. "You know I charge you $20," VonEric answered. "Not for me. For him," she replied. "Oh, $30 for him, too. But he gives me $40." VonEric responded. Kerrington opened her wallet and pulled out three crisp $20 bills. "$20 is for

me, $40 is for him. Tell him if he wants to know who paid for his haircut, he'll meet me at Ocean Prime tomorrow at 8 pm." "Daaaaaaamn, KJ. You coming like dat??" VonEric replied as he took the barber's cape off her. "VonEric, you better not say shit. You better not tell him anything other than what I just told you to say. If I find out you did, you WILL be cutting hair with your feet, because I'ma break all 10 of your fingers!" Kerrington said, demandingly. "Got damn. You need a hug. Or a role model. Or something! Violent ass." VonEric responded. You doing all this threatening; you coulda at least left a tip!"

Chapter Five

As Kerrington drove home from showing a property Saturday afternoon, she couldn't help but wonder to herself if she had done too much in her pursuit of Joaquin. Her thought process is interrupted by the ringing of her phone. It's a group facetime from Lindsey and Shae.

She answers, "Hello, ladies." Shae's face immediately frowns. "Uh uh, bitch. You ain't at work no more. You can stop acting white now." Kerrington laughs. "What the hell do y'all want? I can't drive AND look at you two." Lindsey answers, quickly. "So, a little birdie told me there was some information exchanged yesterday at the shop. I'm just trying to see what was said." Kerrington rolls her eyes. "Bitch, ain't shit little about Shae big mouth ass." Shae, shocked, fires back, "Don't do me, ma'am. I'm 227 lbs. And ALL this weight goes to three places." "Yep…" Kerrington replied. "Your face. Your mouth. And your forehead." Shae smirks and replies softly, "Yo daddy like it."

Lindsey, clearly fed up with their friendly verbal jousting, intervenes to restore order. "Ladies, please. Focus. Kerry has some tea for us." Kerrington tried not to smile but wasn't able to corral her feelings at that moment. She tells them about the conversation she had with VonEric. "Y'all…I did something. And I'm not sure what I think of it." She shared. "Bitch! Out with it!!" Lindsey clamored. Kerrington begins to explain to her friends how she paid for Joaquin's haircut and secretly invited him to dinner Saturday night. "Damn, Kerry." Shae said. "The book said shoot your shot. It didn't say nothing about tricking." "Shae, I know. I've been thinking about it since yesterday. I'm out here looking thirsty all because some stupid ass book told me to take destiny into my own hands. I just feel like I did too much, or maybe I'm coming on too strong. What if he doesn't like aggressive women?? Ya know what? I'm finna call VonEric and tell him don't even worry about delivering that message to him. This is crazy."

Lindsey cuts Kerrington off before she can continue. "No, ma'am. You will do no such thing. Kerrington, you are about to go on a date with a man that literally gave you butterflies the moment you laid eyes on him. Paying for his haircut and inviting him to dinner is just letting him know how serious you are. You said Von told you that he was looking for you that entire night, right?? Stop being over-analytical. You worried about him not liking aggressive women. HA! I tell you what men do like…a woman that knows what she wants! And you're not being aggressive. You're being assertive."

And just like that, Lindsey had talked Kerrington off the ledge. And again, Lindsey was the voice of reason. "You right, friend. I'm really overthinking this." Kerrington said. "You are, Kerry. Your only job now is to show up looking fine as hell and smelling even better. The rest will take care of itself." Lindsey replied.

"Wah…you gonna answer that?" VonEric asked Joaquin as he was putting the finishing touches on his haircut. "Nah, bruh. It's just LeSean. She probably just wants me to come over tonight. I really don't feel like being bothered with her." Joaquin

Chapter Five

replied. "You damn sure don't, 'cause you got plans

tonight," VonEric said. "Oh, word? We going to The

Spot tonight?" Joaquin asked. "No, sir, we are not.

You got a date." VonEric said while taking the barber

cape off." Joaquin looked up at VonEric, confused,

then addressed his comment with a straight face.

"Listen, homie…I have no issue with finding another

barber. You can't be this close to me and

having these kinds of thoughts, nigga." "Boy, stop. I

damn sure ain't talking about me." VonEric said

while laughing.

"Someone has invited you to dinner tonight."

"Bro, what are you talking about?" Joaquin asked,

eagerly. "Tonight at 8 pm, sharp, you need to be at

Ocean Prime. You, my man, have a date." VonEric

explained. Confused, Joaquin asked again, "Von,

what are you talking about, man? Who do I have a

date with??" "I'd tell you, but I need my feet for walking, not cutting hair," VonEric answered. Joaquin is even more confused. "Man, listen. Just do as I'm instructing you. Go home, throw on something nice with some smell good and have yo ass at Ocean Prime at 8 pm. You can thank me later."

Puzzled, Joaquin stands there for a second and then hands him two $20 bills. "You good, homie. She took care of that already." VonEric said with a smirk. "What?? You serious?? Someone paid for my haircut??" Joaquin asked shockingly. "Yes, bro. She paid for the cut, WITHOUT a tip. But go home and get ready. I expect a full report on my desk in the morning." VonEric replied.

Joaquin raced home to get ready for his date with the "secret" lady. His mind was going a hundred miles an hour. Who could it be? What did she look

Chapter Five

like? Where does she know him from? Does she have all her teeth? He didn't know what to think, but he did know that you don't get a second chance to make a first impression. So, he had to make sure he was fly as he could possibly be without overdoing it. When he got home, he wasted no time getting himself together.

Black blazer? Check.

Black button-down shirt? Check.

Black slacks? Check.

Black Bayne Girotti dress shoes? Check.

White handkerchief w/ black polka dots? Check.

Stud earrings? Check.

Watch? Beaded bracelet? Gold chain?

Check. Check. And check.

Chapter Five

Joaquin hit himself with a few sprays of Bond No.9 cologne, and he was out the door. He found himself pushing his Range Rover towards 100mph without even noticing. Excitement had taken over, and anxiousness took the wheel. He had one more stop to make, and he'd be at the restaurant at 8 pm on the dot.

Kerrington sat in an empty area of the restaurant alone. Nervous. Still second guessing herself and the bold move she made. She started to wonder if VonEric even delivered the message. And then she could hear Lindsey's calming voice assuring her that she had done the right thing. "Ok, Kerrington. Calm down. This is just another date with another guy. Stop acting like you're a 12-year-old little girl," she said as she sipped some wine. Then she heard her waiter from around the corner.

Chapter Five

She looked up, and there was Joaquin. Dressed in all black, holding a single, long-stemmed red rose.

Joaquin froze. He could no longer hear the waiter due to sound of his heart beating through his chest. The mystery lady had turned into a dream girl. His dream girl. Kerrington sat there, literally glowing. The strapless red dress she wore complimented her skin. She stood up and time stopped. Alexa, play *There U Go* by Johhny Gill. Kerrington came from around the

table, and he quickly found out how much that dress complimented every curve on her body. He took his time to quickly observe and admire everything about her that was in eyeshot. From her crisp edge to her perfectly manicured white toes. The anklets on both ankles. The six-inch, open-toe, red strapped heels. Her nude-colored fingernails. Her lip gloss that was painted on her lips that was attached to the most radiant smile he had ever seen.

"Wow, so you just bought me one rose? Kinda thought I was at least worth a dozen." Kerrington said as Joaquin walked towards her. "Eh, you don't give up the dozen until you're sure about her," Joaquin said while smiling and handing her the rose. "Well, thank you anyway. It's beautiful." Kerrington said. Looking Kerrington directly in her eyes, Joaquin replied, "It sure is."

Kerrington and Joaquin ate and talked for almost 3 hours. About passing one another in the barbershop, who Korey was, who LeSean was, the whole club incident. Everything. "Business must not be what it used to be in here," Joaquin said. "What makes you say that?" Kerrington asked. "We've been talking for almost three hours. There hasn't been

Chapter Five

anyone else back here. That's crazy for a Saturday night." Joaquin answered. "Oh, their business is fine. I just kinda rented this area. The owner owed me a favor." Kerrington explained. Joaquin sits back in his seat shocked. "So, you had the owner section off a part of his restaurant on a Saturday night just so we could have a date?? You hiding a body for this muthafucka??" Joaquin asked jokingly. "No, silly. You meet a lot of people in my line of work. I've helped him get other properties in the city. Connections are important." Kerrington said. "Wow. WOW. You're something else. For real. You really know how to make an impression on a man." Joaquin said.

Kerrington briefly looks up and smiles at Joaquin. Joaquin waves for the waiter. "You done eating?" He asked. "Come take a ride with me."

Chapter Five

Joaquin paid for the dinner and drove Kerrington to an area high above the city staring directly into the Dallas Skyline. He got out of the truck, grabbed a large, thick blanket from the back, and laid it on the hood and windshield. He removed Kerrington's shoes, picked her up, and laid her gently on the blanket. He took his shoes off, hopped on and lay next to her. She admired the view and listened intently to the music that was still playing inside the truck. Sebastian Mikael's *"Time"* serenade them both.

I can spend all day out if you want

I can take you places, wanna come?

I can spend all until you're down

Cause for you I got time, time, time

Chapter Five

Kerrington managed to break away from the trance Joaquin's cologne had her under and asked him a question. "Don't be alarmed by this; I'm not crazy. Just want your opinion. Do you believe in soul mates?" Joaquin smiled a bit and took his time before answering. "I believe that two people can be placed on this earth specifically for one another. No one else. That person for you and you for that person. The problem is finding that person. And when you do, labeling such a divine union as soul mates just don't pay it the proper respect." Kerrington removed her eyes

from the skyline and onto Joaquin. "Well, what would you call it?" she asked. Joaquin turned and looked at Kerrington and answered. "Destiny."

We ain't gotta ever see the sun

Got everything to turn you on

We can go all day until you're down

Cause for you I got time, time, time

Chapter Six

"The connection is like nothing I've ever experienced. It's like he knows me without me even having to tell him about me. He knows what to say, what to do, and how to do it. He knows when to apply pressure and when to ease up. He truly lets me be me. I'm not saying he's perfect, but he just seems perfect for me." Kerrington can't help but gush over the chemistry between her and Joaquin. The ladies sit at an outdoor brunch spot and listen eagerly as she details their short journey.

"Kerry, if he's perfect for you, then he is perfect. PeriodT," Lindsey said. "That's what I'm saying, Lindsey," Shae added. "Perfection is in the eye of the beholder. And your opinion is the only one that matters, hunny?" she continued. "These last two and a half months have flown by. Every time I see him, it's like the first time. The feeling I get is really indescribable." Kerrington said. "Whew, chile…it's the smile for me! Kerry, you are literally glowing!" Shae said. "Hold on…wait," Lindsey said as her suspicion started to rise. "You start showing all 32 when you someone brings his name up. You over there glowing like that little boy from The Last Dragon. Kerrington Janel Jones!! You fucked that man!!" Lindsey asserted with a loud whisper. Shae hits Kerrington on the arm. "Bitch! You been holding out?!" Shae yells.

Kerrington laughs, and then a subtle calm comes over her face. She takes a long, deep breath and closes her eyes as if she is channeling the experience all over again. "I've never been touched that way before. That man took his time, you hear me!? Nothing was left un-kissed. My body released in ways I didn't know it could. Over and over and over. And just when I thought I had nothing left to give, he talked me through another one. I can't believe I'm saying this, but he knew my body better than I did. It's like he was introducing my body to an entirely new world of

pleasure all while continually pleasing me in ways I didn't know existed. He kept telling me to relax and trust him, and the more I did, the more euphoric the feeling was."

Lindsey and Shae sat in silence as Kerrington came back to reality. Shae turns around and taps the man behind her on the shoulder. "Excuse me, do you have a cigarette?" she asked. "Turn yo self around! We can't take you nowhere!" Lindsey says as she grabs Shae by the arm. "Lawd, I may need to go to the little girl's room. Joaquin been reading them Zane books." Shae says jokingly while fanning herself. "I hate to have to borrow against my 401k, but I need to buy one of them," Lindsey said. Confused, Kerrington asked, "Buy a what?" "To buy a Joaquin." Lindsey answered as they all laughed.

"KJ, I couldn't be happier for you. After that last bum ass, lying ass nigga, you deserve this." Lindsey stated. "Lindsey is right, friend. I can't think of a person I know who deserves to be happy more than you. I cannot WAIT until the day comes when my face lights up when I talk about my man. Wait...That is your man, right?" Shae asked. "No, we both agreed to take our time with this,"

Chapter Six

Kerrington replied. "That book you gave me has really opened my eyes to dating the *right* way, and we don't wanna mess this up. But we're on the same page," she added. "Good," Shae responded. "Cause I need someone to give me hope, and you and him are all I got right now." "It'll come, friend. Just keep being patient." Lindsey said. "I'ma start letting him train me next week. Maybe I can find out if he got a brother or something." Shae said with a laugh. "Girl, listen, he don't play NO games when it comes to his clients, so I hope you're ready because he is going to challenge you in ways you couldn't imagine," said Kerrington. "But I gotta run, ladies; I have a house to show. I'll get with you guys later."

Kerrington rushes off for the home showing appointment. She likes to be early just to make sure

Chapter Six

everything is in place, and the showing goes as smoothly as possible. Kerrington arrives, opens the door, and the front living area is filled with dozens of red, long-stemmed roses. Kerrington is shocked and can't believe what she's seeing. "Where in the hell did all of these roses come from?" she asked aloud. There isn't much room for her to walk through the sea of roses, but she sees a large card on top of the fireplace mantel. She opens the card, and it reads:

I'm sure about her.

-Joaquin

Kerrington's mind immediately went back to her first date with Joaquin and the joke she made about the single red rose. She knew exactly what he meant, and tears started to well up in her eyes. She

Chapter Six

knew she had to get herself together before the client arrived, so she rushed into the bathroom to get herself together.

As she adjusted her make-up, her phone rang. It was a facetime from Joaquin. "Hey, perfect face. Why are your eyes red? You been hitting dat loud??" he asked playfully. "No, silly ass boy. You know why my eyes are like this. Joaquin, this is so sweet!! Thank you, baby!" Kerrington says as she wipes her eyes. "You're more than welcome. I'm glad you like em." He replied. "No, baby. It's not just them. Don't get me wrong, I love the roses, but I'm talking about what you did. Baby, this is amazing! How did you know I was showing this property today?" Kerrington asked. "I knew because you're showing it to me. I called your job and asked that Kerrington

Chapter Six

Jones specifically show this property at this time."
Joaquin explained.

Tears started to form in Kerrington's eyes again. She was overwhelmed with emotion. "This is the nicest, most thoughtful thing anyone has ever done for me. Thank you so much." Kerrington said while wiping her eyes. "Again, you're welcome," Joaquin responded. Kerrington placed Joaquin on hold to check a notification she had just received. It was a $100 cashapp from Joaquin. "Baby, why did you just send me $100?" she asked. "I know that place is a bit a far, and I didn't want you to feel as if I was wasting your time. I know how you are about your work, so that's just gas money. But listen, I gotta jet. Groove is coming in for a session. I'll check in with you later, ok?" Kerrington smiled, and she replied and hung up. She walked back into the living area and stood there momentarily, soaking in and appreciating what she was looking at. She knew she had to repay the gesture that Joaquin went out of his way to make, and she knew just what to do.

"My booooy, what's happening?" Groove said as he greeted Joaquin. You ready to get it in?" "Yes, sir," Joaquin said as they exchanged a brotherly handshake and embrace. "So, how did the flowers work out for you?" Groove asked. "Bruuuuh, couldn't have worked out better. I just got off the phone with her. She was in tears, bro!" Joaquin said excitedly. "What!? Tears?! My man! I can't wait to try on somebody. I'm getting them cheeks fa sho!!" Groove said. "Nah, nigga. Be creative. Get your own ideas." Joaquin responded.

"Damn, my nigga. It's like dat? You must really be feeling Ms. Kerrington?" Groove asked. "I am, bro," Joaquin answered. "You know, I've been around the block a few times and met my share of women, but I've never met anyone like her. I keep trying to find the words to describe her or what I'm feeling, and I can't," he continued. "Wow. You mean to tell me she has

you speechless?" Groove asked. "Yes," Joaquin answered. "Nigga…dat thang must HOT!! She made you forget about LeSean's crazy ass. I haven't heard you mention her in weeks." Groove said while laughing.

"Speak of the devil, and she shall appear. This her crazy ass calling now. She actually chilled for a minute, but this is her fifth time calling me today. And it's barely noon." Joaquin stated. "I guess even crazy has to take breaks." Groove added. "Nah, homie. Her crazy takes NO days off. It just feels really good to get away from that shit. I only told you and Von some of the crazy shit she did." Joaquin said. "Well, tell away, my brother. We got an hour and a half." Groove said as he sat on a weight bench. "Bruh, she had security cameras INSIDE the crib. Just to see if I was on my phone texting while she wasn't around. She waited till I went to sleep once and shared my location with herself. I came outta my mom's crib the next day, and there she was in the driveway waiting. Asking 'what bitch was you in there with', man??" Joaquin explained. "Bruh, she showed up at mom's house?? Man, that's crazy disrespectful. That's grounds for termination of employment." Groove said.

Chapter Six

"Man, who you telling? That's why I'm so glad to be away from her. I ain't thought about her ass one time. Being with Kerry this last month has me seeing life totally differently, man. Sometimes you deal with someone for so long you begin to think their toxic behavior is the norm because you get so use to it. You forget there's better out there. Kerry has reminded me that not only is there better but there's exceptional." Joaquin said as his mind drifted back to Kerrington. "Nigga using big words like he just got outta prison and shi,." Groove said while laughing.

Joaquin and Groove continued to converse and share a few laughs before their session ended. Joaquin went home to catch a Dallas Mavericks game on tv. While he was driving LeSean continued to call, and he continued to ignore her calls. He knew he would have to talk to her eventually and completely break things off as things got more serious with Kerrington. He gets home and takes a quick shower, only to be interrupted by the constant ringing of the doorbell. He already knew who it was.

"LeSean, what the fuc…LeSean, what's wrong??" Joaquin opens the door and sees LeSean crying incessantly. "Fuck you, Joaquin! Fuck you! You been running around with that lil' bald-headed bitch and won't even answer my fucking calls!!" LeSean said, still crying uncontrollably. "LeSean, come in and sit down so we can talk about this." Joaquin pleaded. LeSean began swinging wildly and hitting Joaquin, and yelling at him. "Now you wanna talk?! I had to come over here just to get you to talk to me!! Fuck you, Joaquin!" she yelled. Joaquin tries to grab and hold her to keep her from hitting him.

Chapter Six

"LeSean, calm down. Why are you so fucking angry??" Joaquin asked as he finally corralled her into his arms. "Because I'm pregnant, Joaquin! I'm fucking pregnant…"

Chapter Seven

"**B**IIIIIITCH!!! I'ma have this man's baby if he keeps playing with me like this!!" Kerrington said as she gushed over the rose-filled living room she walked into. "And I can't get a nigga to buy me a damn tulip, and here you are with a car full of roses. Chiiiiiiiile." Lindsey says on their facetime call. "Lindsey, this man even gave me gas money for the trip over here because he said it was taking me away from my work. Like, who is this thoughtful?? Who thinks this way?" Kerrington asked. "Uh uh, I know that look. You got something up your sleeve. What do you have planned, Kerry?"

Lindsey asked. "Giiirl, you know me too damn well. I made a phone call or two and got him an autographed Mavericks jersey by the entire team." Kerrington said. "Awww, Kerry. That is so sweet. He's going to love it." Lindsey replied.

"I really hope he does. I actually had that jersey signed before he even did any of this. He just makes me want to make him happy. Have you ever met a man that you just want to submit to? I mean be completely submissive to him. Lawd, this man just...ugh! I couldn't have designed a better man." Kerrington said. "Kerry, don't you think for one second that this wasn't meant to be. I really wish you could see yourself. I've never seen you smile this hard for so long. Enjoy this, friend. Enjoy HIM!" Lindsey said. "I am, Lindsey. I promise you I am. And I'm going to make sure he enjoys ME! I'm going to cook his favorite meal tomorrow, light some

candles, I'm going to bathe him, and then I'm going

to turn into his personal playground. He's going to

forget I even got him that damn jersey." Kerrington

said with a laugh. "Yes. Ma'am. Reel his ass in!! I

love it!!" Lindsey shouted.

Kerrington eventually got off the phone with

Lindsey and started planning her surprise evening for

Joaquin. She went to the market and grabbed all the

items she needed. She then went

and bought some sexy lingerie that left the mind little

to wonder about. And then she went to get the

autographed jersey framed. Kerrington was beaming

with excitement. She walked out of the framing shop

and thought to herself that this night was going to be

perfect, and absolutely nothing could change that.

Chapter Seven

Joaquin sits in the living room on his sectional couch. Stunned. He stares aimlessly at the flat-screen television that's mounted on his wall. He tries to gather himself as his mind jumps all over the place. There were so many questions, but not enough answers. How did he let this happen? What was he going to do? Should he sue Hennessy? And more importantly, what was he going to tell Kerrington? How was he going to tell Kerrington? Things were going so well between them. He had just told her nothing was going on between him and LeSean, and she was in the past. His mind was racing, only to be interrupted by the doorbell. He was afraid to answer based on what had just happened earlier, but then he remembered he had invited Groove and VonEric over to watch the game.

Chapter Seven

"What's up, bruh? You look like death." Groove said as he walked in. Joaquin walked back to the couch and sat motionless in the same spot. "Say, buddie…why is it so dark in here? You trying to have a séance?" Groove asked. VonEric notices Joaquin not answering and senses something is off. "Wah, you good?" he asked. Joaquin continues to sit motionless. "Hey, you alright, bruh? What's going on??" he continues to ask.

Joaquin takes a deep breath as he sits back and tries to wipe the anguish away from his face and then finally responds. "LeSean." Groove and VonEric both look at each other, confused. "Awww shit, this bitch finally lost what was left of her mind. What she do? Cut all the ass outta

your drawers?" Groove asked. "She's pregnant." Joaquin answers. "Heeeellllll naw. No, bruh!

NOOOO!!!" VonEric yells. "Wah, tell me you fuckin' playing. PLEASE tell me you fuckin' playing, bro!" Groove begged. "Nah, bruh. She just left. Said she pregnant." "Is it yours?" VonEric asked. "Nigga, she ain't stop by here just to tell me she's pregnant by someone else. Hell yea, it's mine."

"Damn, man…what are you gonna do?" Groove asked. Joaquin sat in silence for a moment and answered. "I'ma see it through." Groove and VonEric are both stunned. "Nigga, see what through?" Groove asked aggressively. "Man, I'ma see it through. I'ma see if she and I can work things out and be together for the baby." Groove responds quickly. "I give it four weeks. Tops." "Bro, are you fuckin' serious??" VonEric asked. "You're really trying to be in a relationship with this girl? You do know you can co-parent, right?" VonEric continues.

Chapter Seven

"Nah, man. Fuck dat shit. Ain't no co-parenting. My child isn't gonna grow up being passed back and forth on the weekends just because the parents are stupid and can't get along. We're going to make this work. We didn't have dads growing up. All three of us! My child not going through that shit." Joaquin said.

The room grew quiet as the emotions simmered down. "Bro, listen, you're emotional right now. Just sleep on it before you make any final decisions." VonEric said. "I know, bruh. My mind is just all over the place right now. I know y'all just looking out for me." Joaquin replied. "What did Kerrington have to say?" Groove asked. Joaquin looks up with as much despair on his face as Anthony Hamilton has in his voice. "I haven't told her." At the

Chapter Seven

same time, in unison, VonEric and Groove respond:

"Oh shit!"

Joaquin spends the rest of the evening alone.
Trying to make sense of everything that's happened.
VonEric did bring up a good point about co-
parenting, but the thought of that simply rubbed
Joaquin the wrong way. The thoughts of seeing his
mother struggle to raise him started to set in. He
wondered how much of his life would be different
had his father been around to help raise and support
him. He wondered could the baby actually help he
and LeSean grow up and mature quicker? He knew
VonEric was right; he didn't need to make a decision
tonight. So, he went to bed, hoping he'd have a better
solution the next day.

Chapter Seven

Kerrington was elated. She couldn't wait to see Joaquin and get their romantic evening started. Joaquin had already texted her and said he was on his way. She double-checked everything to make sure everything was perfect. The meal she prepared was simmering on the stove. Her dining room was dimly lit by a few candles that were sitting on the table. She walked in front of a body-length mirror in the living room to give herself one last look over. She wore a thinly strapped, black maxi bodycon dress and some black Steve Madden open-toe heels. She applied an extra coat of lip gloss as she heard the doorbell ring.

She opened the door and greeted Joaquin with the biggest embrace. He kissed her on the cheek and took a seat on her sofa. "Wow, you look amazing. What's all this for?" he asked as he took a look around. "Thank you, baby. Well, you did something nice for me, and now I wanna do something nice for you." Kerrington went into the other room and reappeared, holding the framed jersey she had gotten for Joaquin. His eyes lit up with joy once he saw her come from around the corner. "Bae, are these autographs from the players??" Kerrington smiled and nodded

as she stood behind the frame while still holding it. "You cannot be serious!! WOW! You are truly something else, bae. Thank you!"

Joaquin stood up and hugged and kissed Kerrington. He looked her in the eyes for a moment as he still held her in his arms. "You are just too good to me, and you might be too good for me." He said softly as he let her go. "Sit down, I wanna talk to you for a second." Joaquin grabbed her by the hand and led her back to the sofa. Kerrington could tell the mood had changed. "What's the matter, baby?" Joaquin cleared his throat as he searched for the words to say. "I think we need to chill on each other for a minute." Kerrington was numb. She wanted to speak, but words wouldn't come out. "I have some unfinished business I need to take care of, and I don't think I can do that and continue what you and I have going on."

Kerrington stood up and walked over to the bar. She poured herself a glass of wine, took a sip, and paused. "Unfinished business, huh?" she asked. "Yea, just some unfinished business," Joaquin replied. A smirk came across Kerrington's face, and she took another sip of wine. "LeSean...wow." A look of solemn guilt came across Joaquin's face. He nervously rubbed both of his thighs and prepared to speak. "Kerrington, this is just something I have to do. I wish I could explain it better, but I can't right now.

Kerrington throws the glass of wine at Joaquin. "Just something you have to do?!? You told me that shit between you and her was DEAD! Now you sit your long head ass in MY living room and tell me *'It's just something I have to do.'* Nigga, fuck you! There's something else your lame ass has to do, and that's GROW THE FUCK UP!!" Joaquin removes the glass from his lap and wipes some of the wine from his face. "Look, I thought you'd be a little more mature

than this, but clearly, I was wrong. Kerrington, I didn't wanna hurt you. I really care about you. A lot. But I gotta do what I gotta do." Kerrington quickly fires back. "Mature?? MATURE?? Really, Joaquin! You coulda left me where you found me. You did all of this for what? All because you wanted to fuck me?? Nigga, what you need to do is get the fuck up and get the fuck outta my house. You played me, Joaquin. And I woulda never thought in a million years you were even capable of doing this to me."

Joaquin stands up and pulls his keys from his pocket. "Kerrington, that's not true. That's not true at all. You know better than that. I'm sorry. I truly am. I didn't play you. Some things just happen that are out of your control sometimes." Kerrington nods her head in agreeance. "You're right. Like this."

Joaquin looks at Kerrington in disappointment. Kerrington stares back in disgust. As Joaquin motions towards the door, Kerrington drops a bomb on him. "I thought I was starting to fall in love with you." Joaquin takes a deep breath, turns around, and faces her. "I KNOW I was falling in love with you," he said softly. "But sometimes, love just ain't enough. Goodbye, Kerrington."

Kerrington continues to stand at the bar, trembling. Her eyes start to water. How could something so right go so wrong so quickly? She wonders how did she go from thinking this man was her destiny to throwing a wine glass at him? Kerrington slides down the side of the bar. With her voice starting to crack, she asks herself, "Why does this always happen to me?" She tries to hold back tears and stop herself from shaking, but she can't. The feeling of emptiness overcomes her. How did the man of her dreams place her squarely back into this nightmare?

Lindsey was right, Joaquin was perfect because he was perfect for her, and as she sat on the floor leaning

Chapter Seven

up against that bar, she knew she reacted the way she did because she knew she'd probably never find perfect again.

Joaquin drove home with a million a one emotions flowing through his mind. He wanted to call his brothers and tell them what just happened, but a part of him didn't feel like talking to anyone. As he raced up the freeway, he asked the same question repeatedly, "What have I done?"

Chapter Eight

Code Red was called at Kerrington's house the next night. A *Code Red* is when something catastrophic happens in one of their lives. And at that point, all hands are on deck. They drop whatever they are doing, grab as much wine, ice cream, and as much Kleenex as they can find, and immediately make way to the distressed. They decided to pack pajamas, because this may be an all-nighter. The ladies called Kerrington the next day for details about the special night Kerrington had planned for Joaquin, only to find out the night was anything but special. When they arrived, Kerrington was still wearing the same

Chapter Eight

dress from the night before, and *Broken Promises* by Summer Walker was blaring through her surround sound speakers.

"Awww, Kerry. C'mon, baby…get up." Lindsey pleaded to her as Kerrington lay still on the couch. "Get up, KJ. We got you some food. Tacos, wings, ice cream. Whatever you want, boo. But you gotta get up," Shae said as she picked up the remote control to cut down the music. Kerrington continued to lay there, silently and lifeless. Her eyes were red. They couldn't tell if it was because she was crying all night or from lack of sleep…or both. "Kerry, what happened, baby?" Lindsey asked softly as she sat on the floor in front of her and rubbed her arm.

"My soul aches. I'm jus…I'm just tired. He was for me. That man was truly for me. And he chose someone else. How does this happen? What's for me

Chapter Eight

is supposed to be for ME! But why is he with someone else??" Kerrington started to sob. Lindsey's eyes began to water. Shae sat next to Kerrington, pulled her up from the sofa cushion and held her. "It's not even just him walking out the way he did; it's what he took with him. Y'all, I'm not gonna find that again. The feeling I would get when I saw his name appear on my phone. Just for him to look at me would

set my soul on fire! I would get chills every single time that man touched me. Being around him just made me feel like the world isn't as bad as it seems. He just made everything…better."

Shae and Lindsey looked at one another, speechless. Neither of them knew what to say or how to say it. "Kerry, you said he chose someone else. What do you mean? Who did he choose?" Lindsey asked. "LeSean. His Ex." Kerrington can tell by the awkward silence that they don't know who LeSean is, so she jogs their memory. "The bitch who was in the car in front of the club that night." "Are you fucking serious?? I thought he said there wasn't anything going on between them?" Shae asked. "That is what he said. But clearly, he was lying. We went from talking to each other every day, spending ALL of our free time with each other, sharing the most intimate moments I've ever experienced in my life, just for him to walk out on me."

Shae is incensed. "Ooouuuuh, I can't wait to see his super black ass at the gym. I am cussin' him THE fuck out!" Kerrington wipes her eyes and tried to calm Shae down. "Girl, don't. It's not even worth it. If he wants to be with that ignorant bitch, then let him." Shae is having none of it. "No, ma'am. Fuck that. And fuck him! If he knew he wanted to be with

hoe, he shouldn't have taken it as far as he did with

you. Ooouuhhh, I swear niggas ain't SHIT!" Lindsey

gets up and pours all three of them a glass of wine.

Shae continued, "Kerry, I been waiting my whole life

to feel the way you feel about Joaquin. I think about

it every day. When am I going to get the man that's

for ME? And to know you found your somebody had

me even happier for you than you were for yourself.

To see you like this and to hear you say all this stuff,

I should kick his ass!" Lindsey pours more wine into

Shae's glass. "Friend, your heart is just as

big as your titties, and that's saying something, but

leave that man alone. He made his choice. And he's

going to know he made the wrong choice when he

comes crawling back." Lindsey said.

Chapter Eight

"When I found out Devon was still married and was lying to me the entire time, I was furious. Don't get me wrong; I was hurt, too. But I was engulfed in anger. For a long time, I tried to figure out why. Last night, I finally understood. Devon made me angry. I had feelings for him, but not like this. I don't feel anger right now. I feel pain. I'm hurt. And the only thing that can produce this type of pain is love. For the first time in my life, I was in love. I knew it the moment I laid eyes on him. Y'all, if this is what love is, I don't want it. Y'all can keep it…love hurts."

As Joaquin drives to LeSean's condo, he's on a three-way call with Groove and VonEric telling them about the events from last night. "Bro, she had you a jersey signed by the entire team??" Groove asked. "The entire team, bruh. When she opened the door, it was like my heart skipped a beat. I've seen anything so beautiful in my life. But I sat her down and told her what's what. And it was downhill from there." Both Groove and VonEric want more details.

"Ok, so you told her you're going back to LeSean so y'all can be a family and raise the baby?" VonEric asked. "Uhhh, no. Not quite. I just told her LeSean and I have some unfinished business and needed to see where it could go." They both erupt on Joaquin. "Nigga, what the fuck?? Of course, shit went downhill. What in the hell did you expect??" Groove asked. "Wah, why didn't you tell her about the baby?" asked VonEric. "Man, I just couldn't. I couldn't bring myself to tell her I had a baby on the way. If it fucked me up, I could only imagine what it would have done to her."

Chapter Eight

The guys continue to go back and forth until Joaquin arrives at LeSean's house. "Bruh, listen, she gonna think you only wanted to fuck now. Nigga, leaving her to go be with a family that you started BEFORE you even met her is not a bad thing. It's actually pretty fucking noble." Groove explained. Joaquin paused for a second to process what Groove said. "Man, you're actually right. FUCK!! How did I manage to fuck this up, this badly? The ONE time I find true love, I fuck it up." Joaquin said. "Hold on, bruh. You love her?" Groove asked. "Since the first day I laid eyes on her. That woman speaks to my soul without saying words. Just hearing her voice brightens my day. She makes me see things in a light that I've never seen shit before. I'ma be honest witcha, I doubt I'll ever find another woman like her. It wouldn't matter how long I live. But this baby needs a father, and I'ma be the best damn father he or she could ask for, and if that has to come at the expense of me scarifying what Kerrington and I coulda been, then so be it. But I just pulled up at LeSean's crib; I'ma get with y'all later on."

Joaquin hangs up the phone and rings the doorbell. LeSean answers, beaming. "Hey, baby," she says as she hugs and kisses him on the cheek. They had already discussed what they wanted to do moving forward with the baby earlier that morning, so it was no surprise to Joaquin how excited she was to see him. They were finally going to be a couple again.

"You hungry, boo? I was going to cook, but I just got in from work," she asked. "Yea, I can ea,." Joaquin replied. "Good. I just put in an order at True's Kitchen. I'm just gonna go down there real quick and pick it up. I'll be right back." Joaquin sits on the sofa and grabs the remote control. "That's cool. I guess we can talk some more when you get back." LeSean agrees, kisses him, grabs her keys, phone, and wallet, and walks out of the door.

Joaquin can't help but think about what happened the night before with Kerrington and he thumbs through the channels. He pulls out his phone to check his social media apps and then laughs to himself. He remembered the security cameras she had hidden that would secretly record him while she wasn't there. "She probably recording my ass right now, just like she used to do. I told Groove her ass was crazy." As Joaquin continues to thumb through his phone, an idea hits him like a sack of bricks. The security cameras record everything non-stop. So, the night he came in from the club with LeSean would also be recorded. All he had to do was find her laptop so he could pull up the footage from that night. Joaquin quickly jumps up from the sofa in search of LeSean's laptop. He goes from the living room to the dining room to the kitchen. Nothing. He shoots to the bedroom. Still no sign of her laptop. As he sits on her bed, puzzled, he looks up, and there it is! On the floor in her bathroom in front of the toilet. "Who the hell shits with a laptop??" he asked himself out loud.

Joaquin grabs the laptop and sits at the dining room table. He thinks for a moment about what her password could be. "Think crazy, Joaquin. Think crazy. What do crazy women use as passwords?" He says to himself. After trying unsuccessfully a few times, he stops in fear he may lock up the laptop for too many failed attempts. He carefully types in

Chapter Eight

Beyonce. "GOT EM, COACH!" he yells, and he finally unlocks the laptop. He searches her desktop but doesn't find anything. He types in "S" in the search bar, and "Security Camera Footage" immediately appears. Over 100 hundred folders appear, all dated. He goes to the night in question and hits the spacebar to play the video. He skims to the part of the video where he and LeSean walk in together. He sees them kiss as they walk into the bedroom and take each other clothes off. Joaquin stands up from the table in disbelief at what happens next. "What the FUCK?!"

Chapter Nine

Kerrington's mind has been in a daze. Everything is foggy. All she wants to do is lay in bed and let her broken heart heal, but she knows life won't hit the pause button just because heartache and pain are doing a number on her. So, he has decided to get her work week underway. As she's driving to the office, she gets a call from Lindsey. "Hey, boo. How are you feeling?" "I don't even know," Kerrington answers. "But I do know I need to get up and get on with my life. I'll be fine, though." Just as Lindsey is about to speak, Kerrington gets another incoming call.

Chapter Nine

"Hold on, Lindsey; this is the office calling. Hello, this is Kerrington," she answered. "Hey, Ms. Jones. We've received a request from the Langston Realty Group about a property that we have. They asked to meet with you this morning," the secretary said. "Why me?" a puzzled Kerrington asked. "I'm not sure, Ms. Jones, but they requested you specifically. They want you there for 10 am." Kerrington checks her watch. "10 am?! It's almost 9 am. They BETTER be talking money for such short notice. Email me the specifics, and I'll be on my way."

Kerrington pulls up to a beautiful two-story, 5-bedroom vacation home. As she pulls into the huge driveway, a well-groomed, well-dressed, light-skinned gentleman gets out of a charcoal grey Cadillac Escalade with black accents. "Damn, this man is fine!" Kerrington says to herself as she gathers her things to greet him. "Hi, I'm Kerrington Jones, and I assume you're with the Langston Realty Group?" The gentleman approaches and smiles as he extends his hands. "Yes, ma'am. Good morning and thank you for meeting me on such short notice." "Oh, not a problem. Do you want to go ahead and take a tour of the home?" The gentlemen smiled again. "Lead the way."

Kerrington is captivated by his blinding smile; and the scent that greeted her was something she had never smelt before. She admired the definition in his arms. You could see the outline through his blazer. His tapered haircut looked even better than hers. His hair was thick and wavy, with a part cut into the left corner of his head. His skin was flawless, and he had a chin you could crack nuts with,

Chapter Nine

accompanied by a mustache & goatee combo that connected with his 5 o'clock shadow. His eyebrows were full and thick, and his eyes were jet-black. Big enough to get lost in. Kerrington found herself looking at him as they talked during the tour, but not listening to a word he was saying. "This man is absolutely gorgeous," she thought to herself.

"Can I ask what made you request me, specifically?" Kerrington asked as they continued to walk through the home. "Well, I didn't know what other way I could get you alone to converse with you, so the only option was to create an opportunity." Kerrington stops walking. "Oh? Converse with me in regard to…?" The gentleman chuckles. "In regard to introducing myself and taking you on a date." "Wow, ummm, this is very flattering. Believe me. But I'm not interested in dating at the moment. Mr…wait, I

Chapter Nine

never got your name." The gentleman extended his hand again. "Oh, you're right. My manners. Allow me to introduce myself formally. I'm Aasir."

A look of confusion comes over Kerrington's face. "Aasir? As in Aasir Langston? The real estate mogul??" Aasir laughs. "No, no, no. The real estate mogul is the chairman of the company…and my father. I'm his son. The CEO." The look of confusion goes from shock to surprise. "Oh my God! I have read so much about you and your father. He's a real estate giant! He has literally cornered the market in the entire southern region." "Impressive, Ms. Jones. And

you are correct. My father has done well for himself in this business, but he has decided to take a step back and I now run the company's day-to-day operations." Aasir explains.

Chapter Nine

Kerrington interrupts Aasir before he can continue. "How do you know who I am?" she asked. "Well, Ms. Jones, you're a rising star in this business. You've made quite a name for yourself. I saw you at the Southern Real Estate Awards gala last year. I would have approached you then, but I had a situation at that time. But now that I'm free from it, I figured I'd come pay you a visit," he explained. "So let me get this right. You drove all the way from Houston…" Aasir interrupts and corrects Kerrington. "Flew." Kerrington laughs. "Oh, my apologies. You FLEW all the way from Houston just to ask me out on a date?" Kerrington asks, inquisitively. "Correct." Kerrington pauses for a moment to process everything that's going on.

"Mr. Langston…" Aasir interrupts again. "Please, call me Aasir." "Okay, Aasir. All of this is very, very flattering, but as I said earlier, I'm just not inter…," "Kerrington, stop. You're about to tell me how you aren't interested. Probably because you're too caught up in your work or because you're getting over someone and you're just working on yourself at the moment. I get it. But let's not act as if you aren't interested. You've been blushing since we stepped foot in this vacation home. I see it in your eyes. And my father always tells me, the eyes never lie. Fine. Don't let me take you on a date. How bout we do lunch? And you don't even have to call it a lunch date. Look at it as an investment." "An investment?" Kerrington asked with some intrigue. "Yes, ma'am, an investment. In your future." Aasir responded with a slight smile.

"Wow. I can see you don't get turned down very often. You're pretty cocky." She said. Aasir smiled. "You know what you didn't call me?" he asked. "And what is that, Aasir?" Kerrington said with some intrigue. "A liar." Kerrington stood there and thought to herself. "He has a point. I've been blushing since I laid eyes on his fine ass. And how did he know what I was going to say??" "You know what? Fine. I don't want you to have flown all the way up here for nothing." Kerrington responded. "Wonderful! How does noon sound?" Aasir asked. "It sounds like you better make sure I get a return on this 'investment', Mr. Langston."

Joaquin meets up with VonEric and Groove at The Spot for happy hour. "Having a happy hour on Monday's was an ingenious idea, bruh." VonEric says as he stuffs a wing in his mouth. "Tell me about it. People hate Monday's. This just helps them cope with it. Gives 'em something to look forward to when they punch that clock." Groove explains. "What's up, Wah? What you gotta talk to us about?" Groove asked. "Bruh, something's up with LeSean. I just can't figure out what it is. Something's off." "Yea, nigga…she's off. But you knew that already." Groove responded. "Most pregnant women start acting weird when they're pregnant. It's nothing to worry about." VonEric added.

"Nah, it ain't that. Well, she is acting differently. Bro, we haven't argued one time since we agreed to try and be a 'family'. I've never seen this side of her. But that's not what I'm talking about. Groove, you remember when I told you she would record me at her crib when she wasn't there to see what I was doing?" Groove laughs. "Hell yea, that's some of the craziest shit I've ever heard." "Well, those security cameras never stop rolling. So, I went into her laptop to see if I could find the video of the night after the club."

"Wait, why would you wanna see that? You just wanted to see yourself in action, huh?" VonEric asked. "Nah, bruh…well, yea. But nah! I don't remember us having sex that night. I know how I get off that Henny, but I don't remember doing anything with her." Joaquin explained. "Hold on. Wah, are you telling me you think she's lying??" Groove asked. "Nigga, did you find the video?" VonEric asked. "Man, I'm not saying she's lying; I just wanted to see how all of it went down. Thinking maybe it would jog my memory." VonEric and Groove ask simultaneously: "Nigga, what was on the video?!" Joaquin takes a sip of his drink for dramatic pause. "Nothing."

"Dude!! You just said those cameras don't stop rolling. How was there nothing there?" Groove asked. "That's just the thing. The video shows us walking in the crib. Kissing and taking each other clothes off and shit, but then it cuts off. It just goes blank." Joaquin sits at the bar, just as puzzled as he was when he saw the video. "What did she say when you asked her about it?" VonEric asked. "When I asked her about it?? Nigga, are you crazy?? I didn't ask her shit! Didn't I just tell you that things have never been going this well between me and her? Why would I tell her that I snuck into her laptop to watch us have sex just to make sure we actually had sex??' Joaquin fired back.

Chapter Nine

"Wah, if you aren't sure what happened and you're having doubts, yo ass needs to find out what the hell really went on that night," Groove advised.

"I know, bruh. I'ma keep it a buck: no matter what has gone on between LeSean and me, she's never lied to me. About anything. That's just not in her character. I definitely don't believe she's lying to me." Joaquin said. "Man,

I hear you. But if you truly believed that you wouldn't have gone through that laptop to begin with. Who are you trying to convince: yourself or us?" VonEric asked.

Joaquin sat in silence as he processed what his brothers were telling him. Joaquin wondered where this doubt was coming from suddenly. Why was he second-guessing a woman who had always been honest with him? "Damn. You right, bro. I need to figure this out." "You don't just need to figure this out. You need to figure this out and figure this out quickly!" Groove added. "Yep. I need to figure this out…before it's too late."

Chapter Ten

"LeSean, it's been over a month, and we still haven't decided on a name yet. Why are you making this so hard?" Joaquin and LeSean sit in a booth at her favorite restaurant, trying to decide what they want to name their child. "Baby, I know. I just don't be liking the names you pick. Like you really be trying me. You really think I'ma name my daughter Estelle??" "Hold on, Estelle is a beautiful name. That's my grandmother's name!" Joaquin said. "That's just it. Your grandmother. C'mon into the 21st century, Joaquin. We can vote now." LeSean said, sarcastically. "Ha ha, very funny. But what if it's a boy? Vizeon? Really?" Joaquin asked with

Chapter Ten

even more sarcasm. "Uh uh, don't do me. My momma's name is Vivian. Don't play with her!" LeSean barks. Joaquin laughs at LeSean. "I get that you got the name from your mom, but that name sounds like a planet that a Marvel character came from.

"Ouuhhh, you so disrespectful," LeSean said while laughing. "I'm just playing, babe. Not really, but you know. Listen, LeSean, I been doing a lot of thinking lately, and what we're doing just seems right. It seems perfect. I love you, and I'ma love that baby and be the best father any child can have." Tears welled up in LeSean's eyes. Before she can speak, Joaquin slides her a glass of water. "Baby, you been making me drink water all day," LeSean said with a laugh. "You gotta stay hydrated for you and my lil' one!" LeSean took a sip of water and caressed

Chapter Ten

both sides of Joaquin's face. "Baby, this is all I ever wanted. And just like I told you last night, I was willing to do whatever I needed to do or wait however long I had to wait to get you exactly where you needed to be. With me. I love you, Joaquin. And nothing or no one will ever change that." LeSean closes her eyes and gently kisses Joaquin on the lips.

She gets up and heads toward the restroom. As she opens a stall door, the restroom door opens behind her. It's Joaquin. "Joaquin, what are you doing??" she asked. Joaquin stands by the door and stares at LeSean, and then locks the door. "Joaquin, you are so nasty. You really trying to get some in this bathroom??" Joaquin smiles and walks towards LeSean as she pulls him into the stall. LeSean turns around and pulls up her dress. Joaquin then reaches into his back pocket. "Joaquin, why are you getting a condom? You don't need that. Stop playing, and c'mon before someone tries to come in here." LeSean said. "Oh, nah, I ain't reaching for no condom. I trying to get this..."

LeSean turns around to see Joaquin pull out a pregnancy test. "Joaquin, what is this? What are you doing??" Joaquin takes the test out of the box and points it toward LeSean. "I told you this was perfect. Problem is, it's TOO perfect. LeSean, what happened to the recording of us the night this baby was conceived?" "Boy, what in the hell are you talking about? Let me out of this damn stall!" LeSean said as she tried to push Joaquin aside. "No, ma'am. We ain't going nowhere until you piss on this stick or tell me what happened to the video the night we came back to your crib after the club." "Joaquin, you

really finna piss me off. Move." LeSean demanded.

"Nah, I don't think you get it. No one goes

out of this restroom or comes in until I get some

answers." Joaquin explained. "What damn answers,

Joaquin? What are you talking about with this video

shit? And why do you have a damn pregnancy test in

your back pocket??" LeSean asked, clearly annoyed.

"You have security cameras in your home. They run

24/7. I told you I didn't remember shit from that

night, so I figured I'd take a look and see how it all

went

down. But when I looked through your laptop, the

video went blank after we got to your bedroom. So,

explain to me what the fuck happened to that video

or pee on this damn stick. Those are the only two

ways you're getting outta here. You keep saying

you'd do whatever you needed to do for us to get back together. How long have you been planning this?"

"Wooooow, Joaquin. Are you fuckin' serious?? You went through my laptop?? So, you really think I'm lying about this baby?! When have I ever lied to you? When Joaquin?? When have I ever been dishonest with you? Of all the shit you could accuse me of, you really think I'd lie to you about something like this?" Tears started to come down LeSean's face. "When I found out I was pregnant, it was the best and worst feeling I've ever had in my life. Knowing I finally was going to be a mother but knowing the man I was in love with was with another woman. The only reason I told you was because I felt you should know that you were going to be a father. I didn't ask you to leave that girl. You did that shit

Chapter Ten

on your own! I'm a lot of things, Joaquin, but a liar is not one of them. You wanna go back to that bitch so badly that you'd accuse me of lying about THIS?? You are fuckin' despicable. I'll do this shit on my own. Now get the fuck out of my way."

"Okay, so where are you taking me? And I share my location with my mommy, so you better not be trying no funny business." Kerrington said as she applied lip gloss while looking in the vanity mirror on the inside of the visor. Aasir stops at a red light, puts on his seatbelt, and laughs at Kerrington. "You say that every time we go somewhere. You too funny. But remember last night when you said you wanted barbeque from The Pig On Beale in Memphis?" Kerrington pauses and looks at Aasir. "Uh…yea." "Well, we're going to The Pig On Beale in Memphis to get you some barbeque."

Kerrington closes the visor and puts her lip gloss away. "Aasir. That's a SIX-hour drive. Are you really trying to drive SIX hours just for some barbeque??" Aasir laughs. "No. We're not going to Memphis just to get some barbeque. We're going to Memphis because YOU want some barbeque from Memphis. And…who said we were driving?" Kerrington sits back in her seat in disbelief. "Aasir, you bought us plane tickets just because I said I wanted some barbeque??" she asked. "Nope. Wrong again. You don't need to buy plane tickets when you have a private jet at your disposal." "Aasir…wait, wait, wait. Hold on. Are you serious right now? Are we really going to Memphis? On a private jet? To get barbeque?" Aasir pauses for a moment. "Yes. Is that a problem? You don't want barbeque anymore?" he asked. "No. no, no. That's not…. wow. That's not it. It's just…wow. Ok. Ummm. Ok. Cool, we're going to Memphis. But are we staying overnight? I didn't pack any clothes." Kerrington asked, still astonished. "We can stay overnight if you'd like. We can go get whatever you need when we get there."

Kerrington sat in silence for a few minutes. "Everything alright?" Aasir asked. "Yes. I'm just thinking. I told a guy I was dating once that I was hungry, and he looked at me and asked what I was going to cook US to eat. And here you are, taking me to Memphis, on a jet, to get some barbecue just because I mentioned it the night before. Damn." Aasir laughed. "Am I doing too much too soon? I noticed you've been working some really long hours the past few weeks, so I thought maybe you needed a little getaway. When you mentioned the barbecue last night, I thought this would be the perfect opportunity." Aasir explained.

Kerrinngton thought to herself that the only reason she had been working such long hours was to get her mind off of Joaquin. But she couldn't help but notice that talking to Aasir made her feel better about everything. "Thank you. Thank you so much. I'm literally speechless right now. Thank you for even noticing that I've been working so hard lately. I seriously don't know what to say." Kerrington said as they pulled into a parking lot of an empty commercial building. "You're welcome. C'mon, get out. I wanna show you something." Kerrington and Aasir get out of the truck, and he pulls out some keys

Chapter Ten

and opens the door to the empty two-story commercial building. He holds open the door for her to walk in. "Check it out. Tell me what you think," he says as the door closes behind them. "Aasir, this is beautiful. I always pass by this building all the time and never looked into who owns it." Kerrington said as she walked through the plush building. "We own it. Or at least we did. Just got sold today," he answered. "To who?" Kerrington asked. "You."

Kerrington stopped in her tracks and turned around quickly. "You? What do you mean by 'you'? Who is you?" she asked. "It belongs to you. Give me a dollar, and this building is yours. Free & clear." Aasir answered. "What are you talking about?? Give you a dollar for what?" Aasir pulls the keys out of his pocket. "A few weeks ago, I asked you what were your short-term and your long-term goals. You said your long-term goal was to start your own realty group. Well, now you have a building for that group. Kerrington, I talk to you every day. There isn't a doubt in my mind that you can do this. You're bright, knowledgeable, easily self-motivated, and you're hungry. I told you our first lunch was an investment. Consider this getting a return on your investment."

"Aasir, I can't take this. Remember when you just asked if you were doing too much? Ok, now you're doing too much. I don't mean that in a bad way. But this is a lot. We aren't even together yet." Aasir cuts Kerrington off. "Yet! You said yet! So that means you've thought about it!" Aasir says excitingly. "Of course, I have. You're an amazing guy, and I love spending time with you, but this is a bit much." Kerrington replied. "Kerrington, I understand your caution, and I apologize if I've come

Chapter Ten

off as pretentious. But I believe in you. This isn't an attempt to buy you or impress you. I am simply noticing the immense amount of potential you possess and doing my part to ensure that potential is reached. If I can't pour into a strong, Black, ambitious woman if I have the means and the resources to do so, why am I even here?"

On the flight to Memphis, Kerrington wonders if she and Aasir are moving too fast. She then starts to think about Joaquin and how things ended so badly for them. It's been over a month, and they hadn't seen or talked to one another. Although she was on a flight with a man who clearly would do anything her heart desired, she couldn't help but think of Joaquin. Why does love have to be so hard? Was she ever going to experience what she and Joaquin had again? She then wondered if the answer

Chapter Ten

to those questions was right there on that plane with her?

"Nigga you ain't shit. You really trifling as fuck. If yo punk ass was on fire right now, I wouldn't spit on you to put it out." Joaquin looks up only to see Shae standing over him with a serious scowl on her face. "Are you done?" he asked. "Nigga don't question me. You wasn't worth my friend time any-fuckin-way. I hope you and that lil' dusty bitch live happily ever after. You didn't deserve my friend. I wanna spit on niggas like you! And just so you know, she ain't sitting around the house thinking about yo lil' ugly ass. She has moved on to something you could only wish to be. Goofy ass nigga." Shae stood there with a look of disgust on her face, as if she was growing sick just by being in Joaquin's presence.

Chapter Ten

"Ok, now are you done?" Joaquin asked again. "Yes, nigga. I am. Just like Kerrington is done with yo nothing ass." Shae snapped back. "Good. Let's go get some coffee." Joaquin said as he got up off of his exercise mat. "Nigga, I ain't going nowhere with you. Da fuck?" Shae said. "Look, you walked into MY studio and threatened to spit on me after saying you'd rather watch me burn to death than to actually spit on me to help put the fire out. I think that warrants a cup of Joe." Joaquin explained. "It don't warrant shit. You lucky I ain't come in here and kick yo ass." Shae fired back. Joaquin took a deep sigh. "Listen, there are 3 sides to every story. You only have one. There's more to this than you know. Hell…there's more to this than Kerrington knows. Let's go have some coffee and talk. Maybe then you can determine if I should be spat on or beat up. Or both. I have something to say that I guarantee you wanna hear. Trust me."

Shae reluctantly decided to take Joaquin up on his offer. They ended up at a Starbucks around the corner. They sat outside, and Joaquin told her what happened and why. "But Joaquin, why didn't you just tell her that? Why would you keep that from her??" "Because…" Joaquin said, "She didn't deserve that. The last thing I ever wanted to do was hurt her, but I knew telling her I had a child on the way would probably crush her." They both sat in silence for a second before Shae finally responded. "Joaquin, you really don't know how she would have responded. Kerrington is different. She's not like your average female. I'm willing to bet this would have gone very differently had you just told her everything."

Chapter Ten

Joaquin just sat there, staring across the street but not really looking at anything. "Maybe you're right, but we'll never know now. I just can't imagine her being ok with me having a child on the way with a woman I told her I was completely done with." "Joaquin, being ok with something and accepting something are two different things. She probably wouldn't have been ok with it, but that doesn't mean she wouldn't have accepted it." Shae said. "Damn, I never even thought of it like that. Wow." Shae takes a sip of her Frappuccino. "You're a man. When do y'all ever think? She asked. "Man, chill. I just didn't see it that way. I made a mistake." Shae turns and looks at Joaquin with befuddlement. "No, nigga! You fucked up. You withheld information from her. That's just as bad as lying. You literally pushed her into the arms of another man. Joaquin, you fucked this up." Joaquin sat in silence as he soaked in Shae's words. He knew she was right. He was convinced that had he told her everything, things may have turned out differently.

"Shae, you just don't understand, I really thought I was doing the right thing. But hindsight is always 20/20." Shae scoffs. "Hindsight these nutts, Joaquin. Don't nobody wanna hear that. But, congrats on your child. I know your baby momma is just thrilled about how all of this played out." Shae said with a bit of sarcasm. Joaquin dropped his head as his chin hit his chest. "Ain't no baby momma." Shae spits out her Frappuccino. "What?! She's not pregnant??" Joaquin took a deep breath and tilted his head all the way back. "Yea, she's pregnant. It just ain't mine."

Chapter Ten

Shae reaches for a napkin and wipes her mouth. "What do you mean it isn't yours? How do you know that?" Joaquin chuckles to himself. "She tricked me. She's pregnant, but she's not

pregnant by me. There's a guy she was dealing with off and on. It's his baby. The night y'all saw us leaving The Spot was when I thought it happened, because I was drunk. But I didn't remember us having sex that night. I went back to look at the security cameras in her home, but that night the recording was blank. So, I cornered her in a restroom at a restaurant and made her tell me the truth. I wouldn't let her leave until she showed me the video. I passed out as soon as I walked into her room. Nothing happened. She hooked up with dude the next day. When she found out about me and Kerrington,

Chapter Ten

that's when she decided to come to my house crying

& shit. And I fell for it."

"Wait, wait, wait. Hold on. So, you mean to

tell me that you running 'round here trying to be Carl

Winslow, and that baby ain't even yours?? So, you

left my friend alone for NOTHING??" Shae asked.

The only thing Joaquin could do was nod in

agreement. "Whew, chile…it's the ignorance for me.

So, you mean to tell me you dropped your soulmate

for a bitch that was pregnant with another nigga

baby??" Joaquin takes a deep sigh. "Shae, please

don't pile on. I've been beating myself up enough

about this. It's like a bad dream that won't end."

Shae noticed the anguish and despair on

Joaquin's face. She noticed the change in his body

language. "You really did love my friend, huh?"

Without hesitation, Joaquin answered. "Do." Joaquin

Chapter Ten

couldn't hide the overwhelming feeling that he had just fucked up something that could have been very special. "It's cool, tho. She's where she wants be now. I ain't trippin'." Shae interrupts Joaquin quickly. "Naaaaah, my nigga. Don't try to play that sympathy shit. You made that bed, now lay in it. She wouldn't 'be where she wanna be' if you were better at making decisions and wasn't withholding information. Own it, nigga." "Nah, man. Fuck dat! I did what I

thought was right. Y'all women talk big shit about deadbeat ass dads and nothing ass niggas. Here I am trying my best to be both, and I still end up with the short end of the stick!!" Joaquin said as his voice escalated. "Ok, love. Let's weigh this out. On one hand, you have a woman you're in love with and just also happens to be the woman of your dreams, and

Chapter Ten

on the other hand, you have a crazy bitch that doesn't know the meaning of peace. You chose the latter. Own. It." Shae shot back.

Joaquin and Shae sat and talked for hours. Discussing everything from their love languages to long-term goals. A conversation that started with someone being spat on progressed into two people finding out how much they had in common. They both agreed that being happy was at the very top of their list, and Shae agreed, against her better judgement, that she'd help Joaquin get Kerrington back.

Kerrington and Aasir arrive at their suite at The Peabody hotel. It has been a whirlwind of a day for Kerrington. She still hasn't been able to process everything that's happened. The only thing she knew

Chapter Ten

for certain was that she still didn't know. She didn't

know what to make of Aasir and his advances. She

didn't know why Joaquin still randomly crossed her

mind. She still didn't know if she needed space to

figure herself out and what she wanted to do. But she

couldn't let her indecisiveness bleed into what an

incredible day she had just shared with Aasir, so she

decided to enjoy the evening and whatever it

consisted of.

"Hey, I'm gonna take a quick shower to

freshen up a bit," Kerrington yelled from the

bathroom. She turned the water on in the shower as

hot as she could stand it. She undressed as

she watched the steam from the shower fog up the

mirror. She could vaguely see her reflection in the

glass shower door. Kerrington felt sexy. She paused

for a moment to appreciate how it felt to be desired

the way the man in the other room desired her. She got in the shower and quickly lathered herself up with body wash. As she was enjoying the sensation of the hot water removing the soapy suds from her body, she heard a knock at the bathroom door.

"Hey, is it alright if I come in?" Aasir asked. "Sure," Kerrington answered, without looking up, continuing to wash her body. Moments later, she heard the shower door open. She turned around and there stood Aasir wearing nothing. He stepped in and grabbed her bath sponge and washed her back. He then proceeds to clean her breast, her neck, her stomach and her legs. As Kerrington cleans her vagina, he caresses, rubs, and massages her back and shoulders.

As they got out of the shower, Aasir dried her off and led her to the bed. He grabbed her lotion and

Chapter Ten

applied it all over her body. Aasir speaks as he rubs Kerrington's right foot with lotion, "Alexa, play *Kerrington's Place* from my Apple Music playlist." She then hears Kyle Dion's *Stay the Night* croon through the speakers in every corner of the room.

Now the lights are turnin' on and you're about to leave again

But I just wanna tell you "No, don't go"

Won't you stay with me tonight?

You always have to say goodbye

But I need you to know

I want you close…

Baby, don't leave tonight

At that moment, she feels her toes gently slide into Aasir's mouth. He sucks them passionately. He switches to the left foot. Massaging her foot while simultaneously sucking her toes and rotating his thumb on the top of her clit. Kerrington trembles as chill bumps surface all over her body.

Aasir works his way down. Still licking and kissing each part of her leg. He kisses Kerrington gently on the lips as he travels down to her neck. From her neck to her breast. And from her breast to her vagina. He slows down a bit and focuses on her inner thigh. Licking, biting and kissing. Just enough to tease Kerrington. And without notice, Kerrington feels his warm, wet tongue in her love box. He tongue-fucks Kerrington before swirling his tongue around her clit, all while inserting two fingers in and out of her dripping sweet spot. Just as she is about to climax, she feels Aasir raise his head up. He takes off his boxer briefs, and she feels his manhood drop

Chapter Ten

directly on top of her pulsating pussy. The thud of his

dick startled her. As he reaches for a condom,

Kerrington stops him. "Aasir, wait. Wait, please."

Aasir pulls his underwear back to his waist. "What's

the matter? I do something wrong?" he asked with a

high level of concern on his face.

"NO! No, not at all. You're good. Too good,"

she said as she mumbled the last part under her

breath. "I just don't know if I'm ready for this. I

know I should have stopped you when you started.

I'm really sorry. But I…I just don't know if I'm

moving too fast with. Please don't be

upset with me." Aasir laughed as he lay next to

Kerrington. "Upset?? Baby, I'm just happy to even

be here in this moment with you. I should be

apologizing to you. If I've made you feel

uncomfortable or if I'm rushing all of this, I sincerely

apologize." Kerrington laid her head on his chest. "You are the sweetest man alive. Thank you for understanding and not pressuring me. I always feel comfortable with you. But I just want us to take our time." Kerrington said. "Sweetheart, take all the time you need. I have no problem letting you lead. I'm here as long as you want me here."

They lay there for the rest of the night into the morning, talking. Kerrington didn't realise how relaxed Aasir made her feel. She felt at home with him. She was so impressed at how he handled her not wanting to have sex with him and how patient he was with her. She knew she didn't want to abuse his patience, but she did need to figure out what she was going to do, but she couldn't help but think that Aasir made that the decision all the more easier.

Chapter Eleven

"**S**oooo, let me get this right. She IS pregnant. It's just not yours, but she said it is yours just to make you leave Kerrington alone?" Groove asked as he sat back in VonEric's barber chair. "Yea, that about sums it up," Joaquin answered. "And you held her hostage in a restaurant restroom and tried to make her take a pregnancy test to prove that she wasn't pregnant, but then she admitted that she IS pregnant, but by some nigga who she been secretly fuckin' with?" Goove asks. "Correct again," Joaquin said. "And yo dumbass fell for it? WOW." Groove said as he spun back around in the chair.

Chapter Eleven

VonEric stopped cleaning his barber utensils and leaned up against the counter. "Bruh, hindsight is always 20/20, but got damn, Wah. You really let that crazy broad send you through the ringer this time. Shit!" "What would y'all have done? Seriously?? Looking back on it, the signs were probably there, but what would you have done differently? I was stuck, and I'd much rather forget the shit even happened." Joaquin said in defense of his decision making. "I get it. We both do. But you never said you never told Kerrington. That's a game-changer. We both told you to tell her. What are you gonna do now?" VonEric asked. "I gotta get her back, man. Whatever it takes. I heard she's dating some other nigga now, but I really don't care. That nigga needs to know he's only renting her. I'm coming for what's mine." Joaquin said as he stared

Chapter Eleven

through the glass window of the barbershop. "Whoa, hold on there, Captain Save Em'. What the hell makes you think he's just supposed to bow down and move aside for you? The same things you saw in her that made her special are probably the same things he sees. So, unless he is that other nigga that LeSean was fuckin' around with, you got a fight on ya hands, playboy." Groove said so matter of factly.

Joaquin sat and pondered on what Groove had just laid on him. He thought to himself that Groove made many valid points, but he didn't care. "You right, bruh. Everything you said is probably right. But I really don't give a shit. If what you're saying is true and he sees her the same way I do, he'll be willing to do whatever is necessary to keep her…because I'm willing to do whatever is necessary to get her back." Groove stands up and applauds. "Boy, that sounded amazing! What movie did you see that in?" Groove said jokingly. "Go get your girl, man. Damn, what this fool is talking about. But he is right about one thing, don't expect it to be easy." VonEric added.

"I don't expect it to be easy, but like I said, whatever it takes. But, anyway, I got an extra ticket to this Mavs game; one of y'all wanna go?" Groove hops out of the barber chair and grabs his jacket. "Can't, bro. Gotta head to The Spot and get ready for tonight. We got a new lighting system, and I gotta make sure everything is copasetic." VonEric takes off his barber smock and hangs it in the corner. "You know I would, bro, but I got a HAWT date tonight. I finna go in the back now and tell Mrs. Johnson to

Chapter Eleven

lock up for me." Joaquin sits with a staunch look of judgement on his face. "Y'all ain't shit."

The door opens, and Shae walks in. "Hey, fellas." She says as she greets them before walking towards the back. "What's up, Shae. Hey…you wanna go to the Mavs game with me tonight? I got an extra ticket, and these clowns act like they're too busy." Shae pauses for a moment. "They play the Bulls tonight, too. And Zach Lavine is just…uhm. Yep. I'm in. I'll text you the address." Shae walked to the back and Groove and VonEric were stunned.

"Nigga, you wanna tell me what just happened?" Groove asked as he sat back down. "Dude…how are you going to get Kerrington back if you're dating one of her best friends??" VonEric asked. "Relax, we're not dating. She's actually gonna help me get Kerrington back." Joaquin stated calmly.

"How in the hell is she going to do that at a basketball game?? And when did you even get her phone number??" Groove asked. "Bro, chill. She stopped by the studio a few days ago just to curse me out. I was able to calm her down and actually explain to her what happened. We chopped it up for a bit, and she agreed to help ya boy out. Chill. I got this." Joaquin said confidently. Groove and VonEric stared at Joaquin. "Man…I really hope you know what you're doing," VonEric said. Joaquin stood up and reached for the exit door. "I got this."

Joaquin sat outside of Shae's condo, waiting for her to come downstairs. He glanced up from his phone and saw Shae walking through the double doors. He was mesmerized. "Got damn!" Of course,

Chapter Eleven

he had seen Shae before, but not quite like this. She was stunning. Shae was about as physically imposing as a woman could be. 5'9", 190lbs, and radiant, glowing caramel skin. Shae's chest had its own area code, and her ass-to-hip-to-waist ratio was definitely something to write home about. Rarely do you ever see a gorgeous woman, with incredibly large breasts, a small waistline and an ass that would leave any seat warm. He quickly had to snap out of that trance before he made things awkward.

"Damn, nigga. You ain't gonna open the door for me?" Shae asked as she opened the door and climbed in. "Open the door? For what? This ain't no date. Buckle up and sit back." Shae scoffed. "Rude! I know Mrs. Stevenson raised you better." Joaquin laughed as he pulled off and exited the parking lot. "So, have you been thinking about what angle you're going to take to get Kerrington back?" Joaquin took a deep sigh. "Yea, that's all I've been thinking about. I just need you to see if she'll hear me out. Just kinda gauge whether she'd give me the time of day. I'll take it from there." Shae nodded in approval. "I can do that. I'll just ask her if she's spoken with you at all. How she responds will tell me everything I need to know."

"I shouldn't do shit for yo ass the way you treating me." Shae shot off. "Bruh, you still trippin' on that door thing?" Joaquin asked, annoyed. "Yes, Joaquin. I know this isn't a date, but I'm a lady and you should acknowledge me as such. Or any lady, for that matter." Shae responded. "You know what? You're right. I apologize. And let me tell you that you look great tonight, and you smell even better."

Chapter Eleven

Joaquin said. "Now that's better. And thank you."

They finally arrived at the American Airlines arena

and found their seats. They talked about the team and

Joaquin was surprised at how much Shae knew about

basketball. He enjoyed hearing about the sport from

a woman's perspective. It probably wasn't a date, but

the vibe he was experiencing with Shae made it feel

like one.

"So how did you manage to get your own

skybox for Mavericks games if you're from

Houston? Wouldn't that make you a Rockets fan?"

Kerrington asked Aasir as they exited the elevator.

"My pop has ALWAYS been a Mavs fan. He and

Mark Cuban are actually really good friends. So, it

was just kind of natural for them to be my favorite

basketball team as well. I've been around the

franchise my entire life." Aasir explained. "Wow. That's really cute. I love how

you and your father are." Kerrington said. "That's my best friend. He literally taught me everything I know." Aasir responded.

Aasir and Kerrington arrive at their skybox just in time for the game to tip off. They take their seats, and Aasir orders champagne. "Speaking of my pops, he can't wait to meet you," Aasir said. "Wait, are you serious? You told your father about me?" Kerrington asked as she choked on the champagne she sipped. "Of course, it was his idea that I come here to meet you in the first place. I talked to him about you often before we ever met. I knew you were special even back then. Is that bad?" Aasir asked. Kerrington was a bit shocked that a man she had never met was paying so much attention to her without her even knowing. It was flattering. "Oh, no. Not at all. Just surprised you even talked about me to him."

The game had started. The Bulls and Mavericks were going back and forth. Neither team was able to pull away from the other. Kerrington and Aasir didn't do too much watching of the game. They conversed during most of it. Discussing professional plans for the future, among other things. They were just enjoying each other's company. The Bulls called a timeout, and the jumbotron hanging above the arena floor began showing kids in the stands dancing. Then the jumbotron operator turned on the *Kissing Kam,* which highlights couples in the stands, and once the camera is on you, you then must kiss your partner.

Chapter Eleven

The camera found an unsuspecting, nice-looking young couple. The roar of the crowd prompted Kerrington to move her attention toward the jumbotron. There she saw Joaquin and Shae nestled up with one another and Shae applying a fake kiss to Joaquin's cheek. Kerrington was livid. "Hey, can you tell me where the restroom is?" she asked Aasir. She hurried down the

hall and burst through the restroom door. She pulled out her phone to call Lindsey, but she didn't pick up. She called a few more times, but still no answer.

Kerrington felt her body getting hot. She paced back and forth, wondering what to do next. She tried to calm herself down, but nothing was working. She pulled up Shae's name in her phone and just stared at it. She wanted to call, but she didn't know what to say. Why was she at this game with

Chapter Eleven

Joaquin? Why would he betray her like this? Why would SHE betray her like this? How long has this been going on? What the fuck happened to him and that bitch LeSean? So many questions. No answers. Her eyes were starting to water. She got herself together and made her way back to the skybox.

"Hey, is everything ok?" Aasir asked. "Oh, yes. Everything is fine. Hey…are you ready to go?" Kerrington asked. "Now? I mean it isn't even halftime yet." Aasir responded. "Yes. I was thinking we could just grab some food and a bottle of wine, and head back to my place, and watch a movie or something." Kerrington replied. "Oh. You wanna get some wine? And head back to your place?? Sure! No problem." Kerrington's mind was racing, and her heart was pounding. She knew she needed some answers, but she also knew she probably wasn't

Chapter Eleven

going to get them tonight. But what she did know was that she could not spend another moment in that arena without going to jail.

Joaquin drives up the freeway as Shae thumbs through his music library. "Ouuuhhh, this is my SHIT!" Shae screams. She leans forward to increase the volume as Prince's *Insatiable* blares through the speakers. "Say, man…what was that fake ass kiss you gave me at the game??"
Joaquin asked as they both burst out into laughter. "I have no fucking idea. Them people kept getting louder and louder. I had to do something." Shae said while still laughing.

Joaquin pulls up to her building and gets out to open her door. "You learn quickly! I like dat!" Shae said as she climbed out of Joaquin's Range

Chapter Eleven

Rover. Joaquin walked her to the door as they continued to laugh about the fake kiss. "Your eyes got soooo big." Shae said. "Cap! I was calm as still water and smooth as a baby's ass." Joaquin said with a chuckle. "Boy, hush! But anyway, Mr. Stevenson, I really enjoyed you this evening. Thanks for the invite." Joaquin motioned towards opening the door for Shae. "Man, fa sho. I had a damn good time myself."

Unexpectedly, they hugged one another. Shae felt Joaquin's beard brush against her face. Joaquin felt Shae's chest pressed up against his. They both released one another just enough to make eye contact. They paused. Joaquin's subtle hold of Shae's waist became a bit firmer. They stood nose to nose with their top lips less than a quarter of an inch in separation. "So, you wanted a real kiss, huh?"

Chapter Eleven

Shae asked. "I think you wanted to give me a real kiss," Joaquin replied. "Well, if I wanted to give you a real kiss, why haven't I given you one yet?" Shae asked softly. "Because you keep talking." Joaqiun answers. Shae simply replied, "Say less…"

Chapter Twelve

"Good morning", Kerrington said softly as she brought Aasir a cup of coffee. "Great morning! Umm, that is delicious, thank you," he said as he took a sip. "Not 'great morning', Kerrington said with a laugh. Aasir chuckled to himself as he sat up in the bed. "Great morning with an even better night. You definitely know how to make a lasting impression." Kerrington laughs again. "So, I take it that you enjoyed yourself last night?" she asked. "Enjoyed would be an understatement," Aasir replied. "Wonderful. Mission accomplished. I was about to make breakfast, but I wasn't sure on what type of breakfast foods you eat." Kerrington said while opening her curtains. Aasir took another sip of coffee. "Umm, I'm sure whatever you whip up will get devoured. Just like you." Kerrington leans in for a kiss. "Boy, if you want me for breakfast, just say that."

They laugh together as Kerrington rises from the bed to head toward the kitchen. Aasir reaches for her hand. "Hey, can I ask you a quick question?" he said. "Sure, sweetie." Aasir leans over and places the coffee mug on the nightstand. "Don't take this the wrong way, but why the change of heart?" A look of confusion comes over Kerrington's face. "What do you mean?" "Well, just a week ago, I was all over you. And although I could tell you enjoyed it, I could also tell that you weren't all the way into it. What changed in such a short period of time?" he explained.

"Hmmm, I wouldn't say that anything changed for me. There was just something last night at the game that struck me. It felt like the right time, and I didn't want to wait any longer. Aasir, you've been amazing. You've been incredibly sweet and very understanding, and sometimes I get wrapped up in all of that. Well, I think I need to do a better job of showing my

appreciation and matching your energy. Now, by no means am I saying last night was me showing appreciation. It was something I wanted to do, but it was more of me letting you know that we're on the same page." Aasir smiles. "Same page? You do know what page I'm on, right?" he asked eagerly.

Chapter Twelve

"Yea, I do. And I'm letting you know we're on the same page."

"Well, I tell you what, you go ahead and cook that breakfast, and we can discuss this further another time. I'm really enjoying this. I'm enjoying you, and I wanna continue doing that." Kerrington went into the kitchen and prepared breakfast. She and Aasir talked as they ate. They finally had a conversation about how they felt towards one another and what they wanted moving forward. Time was starting to get away from them, so they agreed to reconvene at dinner later that night. Aasir collected his things, kissed Kerrington on the cheek, and left.

Kerrington immediately grabbed her phone and called Lindsey. "Hey, boo…what's up?" Lindsey asked. "BITCH!! Why didn't you answer the phone last night??" Kerrington asked

Chapter Twelve

aggressively. "Damn! A bitch can't get her back

blown out without being interrogated by the Nosey

Committee??" Kerrington began telling Lindsey

what happened at the basketball game the night

before. She told her how she saw Joaquin and Shae

hugged up on the jumbotron and how Shae gave

Joaquin a fake kiss on the cheek on the Kissing Kam.

"Kerry, are you fuckin' serious?? Wait…this is too

much. Code Red. I already have the wine, just hurry

up and brang yo ass over here!" Lindsey instructed.

Kerrington took a shower, got dressed, and zoomed

over to Lindsey's apartment.

She finally arrives and knocks on Lindsey's

door. The moment she opens, Kerrington starts going

off. "And you shoulda saw that bitch…all hugged up

and shit. Like they been in a

fuckin' relationship for 10 damn years. I can't wait

till I see her ass. I'ma…" Kerrington puts down her

purse and her phone and turns around, only to see

Shae sitting on the sofa. "I can't fuckin' believe you,"

Kerrington said to her in her calmest tone. Lindsey

closes the door and interrupts Kerrington. "Hold on,

Kerry. I called her as soon as we got off the phone.

Hear her out." Kerrington scoffs at Lindsey. "I ain't

trying to hear shit this backstabbing bitch has to say!"

Shae stands up. "Kerrington, please listen. It's not

what you think."

Kerrington folds her arms and looks Shae in

the eyes. "So, you're telling me that you two weren't

on a date last night? You're telling me that you didn't

go behind my back and fuck that man?!?!"

Kerrington yelled. "Kerry, that is exactly what I'm

telling you. You are my fuckin' sister. I wouldn't do

Chapter Twelve

ANYTING to hurt you." Shae pleaded. "Well, yo ass failed. Because I know what I saw." Shae interrupts Kerrington. "What you saw was two people hanging out at a basketball game. That's it. It wasn't a date. Kerry, Joaquin wants you back. And he asked me to help him." Kerrinngton laughs. "He wants me back?? Just how in the hell is he going to do that by being hugged up with you at a damn basketball game?" she asked.

"Kerrington, we weren't hugged up. I went to his studio to tell him about himself. When I did, he let me in on something. And that's when he asked for my help." Shae said. "Let you in on what??" Shae pauses for a moment. "You're going to have to ask him that yourself. But he saw me at the shop yesterday and said he had an extra ticket to the game. Groove and Von couldn't go, so that's when he asked me. Kerry, I promise it was totally innocent. That little kiss you saw was bullshit. My lips didn't even touch his face."

Kerrington stands there in silence and continues to process all that Shae has said. "So, you didn't fuck him last night, Shae?" Shae looks in shock. "Are you fucking serious? You'd really ask me that? Hell no!" Shae shot back. Kerrington paused again. "Well, did you kiss him?" Shae looks as if she saw a ghost.

"So, you wanted a real kiss, huh? Shae asked. "I think you wanted to give me a real kiss" Joaquin replied. "Well, if I wanted to give you a real kiss, why haven't I given you one yet" "Because you keep talking." Shae simply replied "Say less..." As their lips get closer to one another, they both stop and say

simultaneously, "We can't do this." Their bodies separate just enough to make eye contact again. "Yea, we trippin'. I love that girl too much to go out like this." Joaquin spoke. "That's my fuckin' sister. I shouldn't even be here like this" Shae said. They both moved back from one another. Joaquin turned and walked to his car, and Shae turned and walked into her building.

"And that's all that happened. We kinda got caught up in the moment. Maybe we were both vulnerable last night, but I promise you, that's exactly what happened. I'm so sorry it even got that far." Kerrington stood motionless for a few moments. "Why in the hell would YOU be feeling vulnerable of all people?" Kerrington asked. "Kerry, I really don't think you get it. I saw how you looked at him. I remember how you would light up just by seeing his name on your phone. I want that! I want to know how that feels! I wanna know how it feels to be in love. It wasn't even Joaquin, last night was really about me just wanting to be in the moment. And I realized I couldn't be in that moment with him. And I stopped it. Immediately."

Kerrington sat down on the couch, visibly frustrated. Lindsey and Shae looked on in silence, not knowing what to say or do. Kerrington finally got up, grabbed her things, and left. She sped all the way home. Her mind was scrambled. She was still upset with Shae, but she didn't know if she was mad her for what almost happened or was she simply mad because she wanted someone to be mad at. Her head was pounding when she got home. She took some aspirin and dozed off for a while. When she woke up,

Chapter Twelve

she saw a text message from Aasir detailing the reservations he set for dinner. Kerrington lit some candles, played some music, and soaked in her bathtub. She replayed the conversation with Shae in her head over and over. She didn't know what to think or how to feel. She wondered what Shae meant when she said. "...*he let me in on something.*" What did Joaquin tell her?

Kerrington finally got out of the bathtub and got dressed. She calls Aasir as she walks out of the door to let him know she's on her way. When she opens the door, Joaquin is standing there as if he's about to knock. Kerrington's heart fell to the bottom of her ass. She froze. This was the first time she had seen him in person since he said he was going to be with LeSean. "Hey…" Joaquin said softly. "…hey," she responded. "Do you mind if I come in?" he asked. "Yes. As a matter of fact, I do. Why are you here, Joaquin?" Kerrington asked sharply.

"I'm here because I want to talk to you." He responded. "About what, Joaquin?" "About us. I miss you." He spoke. "There is no us. You made that abundantly clear the last time you were here." Kerrington said with a bit of sarcasm. "I know. And I was wrong. I made a mistake. Will you please let me in so I can explain?" he asked. "No, nigga, You damn right you made a mistake. And you made another mistake thinking you could come here, and I'd just welcome you with open arms. You hurt me, Joaquin. You hurt me deep in my fuckin' soul. I couldn't eat. I couldn't sleep. I wasn't going to work. I had someone trying to make love to me, and I couldn't let him because the hands that were all over me weren't yours! At first, I was lying to this man and stringing him along all because I couldn't get over you! Half the time I'm with him, I'm thinking about your raggedy ass! But that shit is DONE! You just left me for another bitch. You really…"

"I left you because she told me she was pregnant," Joaquin said as he cut her off. "She told me the night we left The Spot, we had sex, and I got her pregnant." Kerrington was stunned, but she quickly regrouped. "Joaquin, if she's pregnant, why are you on my doorstep?" Kerrington asked. "That's the thing, Kerry. She's not. Well, she's not pregnant by me. She lied to keep me from being with you." Joaquin explained. Kerrington looked into Joaquin's eyes. She could see the desperation on his face. She could hear the sincerity in his voice. And none of that mattered.

Chapter Twelve

"Joaquin, you coulda told me all of that, but you decided to withhold it from it me. In my book, that's just as bad as lying to me. You made your bed, now lay in it. I've moved on, and I suggest you do the same." Kerrington closed her door, locked it, and walked away.

"Kerrington...I love you." Kerrington turned around and responded without hesitation. "...but sometimes, love just ain't enough, remember?!" Joaquin stood there, heartbroken, as he watched Kerrington drive away.

Kerrington arrived at the restaurant to meet Aasir. He was already seated when she walked in. She walks over and kisses him on the cheek. "Hey, baby. Sorry I'm running late. That nap lasted longer than I wanted it to." Kerrington said with a laugh. "A

Chapter Twelve

nap…oh," Aasir said. "Was it the nap that took longer than expected or the conversation with Joaquin?" he asked as he sat back in his chair, rotating an almost empty champagne glass in his hand. Kerrington sat blindsided as she tried to find the words to speak. Aasir holds up his cell phone to show an ongoing call from Kerrington. "You never ended the call…"

Chapter Thirteen

"Hey, where are you?" "I'm sitting in my truck," Joaquin answered. Shae tries to alert Joaquin that she spoke with Kerrington earlier. "Listen, I spoke with Kerrington a little while ago and it didn't go well." Joaquin sits up in his seat. "What do you mean it didn't go well??" he asked. "Well, she saw us at the basketball game. I tried to explain to her what happened, but she didn't seem too receptive to it." Shae said "What do you mean you tried to explain to her what happened? NOTHING happened!" Joaquin yelled. "Right. I know that and you know that, but she did see us all hugged up on the jumbotron." She explained. "Shit! She saw that??" "Yea, and I kinda mentioned that we almost kissed," Shae said, hesitantly. "FUCK, Shae! Why would you tell her that??" Joaquin yelled into the phone. "Because she asked, Joaquin! And I'm not hiding shit from her. That's my damn sister! You should have enough of hiding shit from here anyway! That's how you got in this mess in the first place."

Joaquin calmed down as he realized Shae had made a valid point. "Shit…you're right. I'm trippin'. My bad, man." Joaquin said as he sunk back down in his seat. "Why are you just sitting in your truck?" Shae asked. "Well, your warning was just a tab bit late. I'm sitting outside of Kerrington's crib." Shae gasped. "Oh, Lawd…you hit that stalking stage! Go home, Joaquin. You're better than this!" Shae said.

Chapter Thirteen

"Nigga, I ain't stalking her! We just had a conversation...a brief conversation. Joaquin explained. "Oh, no. What happened." Joaquin took a deep breath and explained to Shae what had taken place.

"I came to let her know what happened. What REALLY happened? And she didn't wanna hear any of that shit. She didn't wanna hear shit I had to say. I told her LeSean was lying about being pregnant by me. Then she told me that none of that shit mattered. I shoulda been

upfront from the beginning. Then she walked off. Probably going to see that other nigga." Shae could hear the despair in Joaquin's voice. "Awww, Joaquin. I'm sorry. I really sorry. You just need to give her some time. She'll get over it." Joaquin quickly interjected. "That's the problem, Shae. I don't have any time. At least not any to waste. The more time that goes by, the closer she gets with dude and the further she gets from me. And I can't have that." Joaquin said as his voice shifted from defeated to determined.

"Wow. You're right. I didn't think of it like that. So, what are you gonna do?" Shae asked. "I'ma go get my fuckin' woman. Women like Kerrington don't come into your life often. Maybe once in a lifetime. I love Kerrington. I'm *in* love with Kerrington. And as long as there is breath in these lungs, I'ma do what I gotta do to let her know this is home and this is where she needs to be."

Kerrington sits across from Aasir, motionless. She plays back in her head when she called Aasir to let him know she was on her way to meet him, but then opening the door and seeing

Joaquin. She never hit the end call button. "So,

you've been lying to me, huh?" Aasir asked calmly.

"Aasir. No. I promise you; it's not what you think."

Kerrington said. "Oh, it's not. Well, explain to me

how in the hell could it possibly be anything else"

Aasir said as his voice escalated. "Aasir, please calm

down. What you heard was me addressing someone

from my past. I admit, when we first met, I wasn't

sure about you, mostly due to me not being over him.

But that's in the past. And that's what I came to talk

to you about tonight. Us. I'm all in on you and me."

Aasir frowned and gave Kerrington a sharp,

piercing stare. "You and me? Us?? Kerrington I've

been all in on YOU since the day we met. My

everything has been YOU. I get headaches trying to

figure out ways to make you happy. To make you

Chapter Thirteen

understand that there is NOTHING I wouldn't do to please you. Dammit, if you wanted the sun, I'd build a fuckin' spaceship and go get it! And if I couldn't get it, I'd make it shine your way." Kerrington tries to find the words that'll help quell what Aasir heard. "Baby, I know that. I'm aware of all of that. Just calm down and listen to me, please. I was emotional, and you took what I said outta context…" Aasir rises up from the table and leans over to Kerrington as he grabs his blazer from the back of his chair. "Let me tell you something. I am Aasir Fucking Langston. I come second to NO ONE. If you wanna be with that fuck nigga, that's your business. But I will not be your rebound nigga. Lose my number and stay the fuck away from me.

Kerrington sits there as her eyes begin to water, and she watches Aasir walk away. She tries to process everything that's happened in the past hour. Her emotions are running rampant, and she can't control them. She rushes to her truck and cries uncontrollably. As she drives home, she can't help but think about Joaquin. Why did he decide to come back into her life now? Why now, when everything was going so well with Aasir? She didn't realize how deeply she felt for Aasir until she saw how emotionally disturbed she was about the events that had just occurred.

She finally got home and undressed quickly. She soaked in her bathtub until the water began to get cold. She began to wonder were her feelings for Aasir legit? Or was Joaquin's sudden appearance at her doorstep too much for her to process, emotionally? She remembered the connection they

Chapter Thirteen

had and how her feelings for him never truly left. She

wondered if she really

just suppressed them with Aasir. Her thoughts were

interrupted by the ringing of her phone. It's Joaquin.

She answers but doesn't say anything. "So,

you still soak in the bathtub when you need to clear

your mind, huh?" he asked. "Boy, how do you know

I'm in the bathtub??" she asked as she began to look

around her bathroom. "I heard the water moving

when you answered the phone. I bet it's starting to

get cold, too, huh?" Kerrington became annoyed by

how well he knew her. "Joaquin, what is it?" she

asked. "I wanna talk to you. Can you meet me

somewhere?" "No, I cannot. I'm really not in the

mood for talking. I just wanna be left alone."

Kerrington explained. "Kerry, I promise I'm not

trying to bother you, but I really need to speak with

you." Joaquin pleaded. "Joaquin. No. I'm not in the mood. The last time you wanted to tell me something, my night didn't end so well. So, I'm good on that. I'm good on you." She spoke. "Oh, word?? You good on me??" Joaquin asked with a high level of intrigue. "Yes, Joaquin. I'm good on you. You had your chance and you decided to push me aside and withhold shit from me. We…"

Kerrington is interrupted by her doorbell. "UGH! Who the fuck is this??" She gets out of the bathtub and quickly grabs her robe. She opens the door, and Joaquin is standing there in some grey sweatpants that are cut off at the knee and a crisp, white muscle shirt. His eyes are gleaming. His skin is shining. Her heart starts racing. "We what?" he asked as he looked her in the eyes. "Joaquin, I don't know who the fuck you think you are, but you can't just be poppin…" Joaquin picks up Kerrington and sticks his tongue in her mouth. Her legs are around his waist, and her arms are around his neck as her hands caress the back of his head.

Joaquin lets himself in as they continue to kiss, passionately. Kerrington sucks his tongue as Joaquin pushes it further into her mouth. He tosses Kerrington onto the bed. He stood and admired her for a second. The moonlight crept in from the partially opened blinds as the light complimented her still-wet body. He missed her. Joaquin wasted no time as he climbed on top of her. He spread her legs and reintroduced himself to her honey pot. Joaquin sucked and licked her pearl tongue incessantly. He would stop and do the same to her inner thigh just to tease her. Joaquin knew her spot. He began to tongue kiss her clit and devour her vagina until she climaxed. Her body began to tremble, and her legs began to shake uncontrollably. Joaquin knew Kerrington's body just as well as he knew Kerrington.

As she continued to shake, Joaquin flipped her over and proceed to lose his tongue in between her ass cheeks. He could hear her attempt to say his name, but the insertion of his tongue produced a pause. He could tell from the crack in her voice that she was pleased with his actions. Joaquin began to squeeze and caress her ass as he kissed and licked the small of her back. She could feel her juices on his beard as he worked his way up her spine. As Joaquin grabbed her by the front of her neck, she could feel his log of a dick resting on the back of her thigh as it grazed the back of her knee.

Chapter Thirteen

Joaquin turned her over onto her back and placed a pillow under her at the bottom of her spine. He reached into her nightstand and pulled out her rose toy. As he balanced her on the pillow, she felt Joaquin work his way into her. He slowly stroked her until he was well into her stomach. He kissed and licked around her calf. He could feel her walls tighten around his dick the deeper he stroked. He placed the rose toy on top of her clit as he stroked faster. He licked and

sucked on each of her perfectly pedicured toes as he. Joaquin stops abruptly and inserts his warm tongue back inside of Kerrington. Her moans grew to cries of pleasure. He could feel her body starting to tremble again, so he rose and slid his massive dick back into her pulsating vagina. Kerrington was in another world. Sexual bliss. She had longed for his touch, for her skin to be next to his. She missed the scent of him.

Joaquin grabs her by the throat, looks Kerrington in the eyes, and says sternly, but softly "You belong to me." Too immersed in the sea of emotions and sexual pleasure, Kerrington could only nod. Joaquin flips her over and shoves his member back inside of her. His slow and steady strokes allow Kerrington to enjoy every inch of him. He firmly grabs her by the neck with his left hand, and grips her waist with his right hand, and begins to thrust harder and harder as he uses his leverage to guide Kerrington's body in a back-and-forth motion.

Kerrington's body cannot take anymore. She screams as an uncaged orgasm brings her to tears. Joaquin stops to let the orgasm run its course. He kisses and caresses her until her body idles down. No

Chapter Thirteen

words are spoken. Kerrington lay on her side as Joaquin held her. She wanted to live in the moment. She wanted to take in everything that had happened. She didn't know what the next day would bring, but at this very moment, none of that mattered. She felt good. She felt amazing. Her soul was fed. And finally, her mind was at ease.

Kerrington awakes from her slumber and quickly notices Joaquin was no longer lying next to her. She grabbed her robe as she exited her bedroom. She smelled food as got closer to the kitchen. To her surprise, there was Joaquin, making omelets for the both of them. "Morning. You look like you could use some protein." Joaquin said with a smile. "Yeeaaa, I could definitely use something to replace all the fluids I lost last night," Kerrington said with a slight laugh. "Well, good. I hope you still like your omelets with spinach and mozzarella cheese?" Joaquin asked as he placed the omelet on a plate and handed it to Kerrington. "Uh, yea. This is perfect. Thank you."

Kerrington sat on the barstool at the island in the middle of her kitchen. Joaquin handed her a small glass of orange juice, along with a napkin, as he sat down to eat, as well. There was an awkward silence that filled the kitchen. They would glance up from their plates and look at one another in between bites. "Listen, we need to talk. Not just about last night, but in general." Joaquin stated. Kerrington paused for a moment. "You're right. I think we definitely need to discuss a few things." Joaquin pushes his plate away. "I know you have questions. Hell, I have questions. We may not even have all the answers that we're

Chapter Thirteen

searching for, but that doesn't mean we can't find them together," he shared.

"Joaquin, what happened last night shouldn't have happened. And to be honest…" Joaquin quickly cuts Kerrington off. "But it DID happen. Why are you putting fate into question? It happened because it was supposed to happen. We fell in love with one another because we were supposed to. You are for me, and I am for you. And there is nothing I am not willing to do to prove that to you." Kerrington scoffed at Joaquin. "So, you think it's that easy, huh? You think you can just dick me down, make some eggs, and I'm right back where I was when we first met, huh? Joaquin, you ain't got that kind of motion, sweetie. I promise you don't."

"Kerrington, how 'easy' this may or may not be has not crossed my mind one single solitary time.

Because I don't care. Whatever needs to be done to make you understand that THIS is where you need to be will be done. Whatever mountain that needs to be moved, will be moved. Whatever is deemed impossible, will be made possible. I just need the opportunity." Joaquin pleaded.

Joaquin walked around the island and turned the barstool Kerrington was sitting on towards him. "How about this: You doll yourself up, slip into something sexy and meet me at my place at 8 pm. I'll cook us some dinner, and we can talk then, cool?" Kerrington stared at Joaquin for a moment. She wanted to play hardball so badly, but she simply melted around him. She slid off the stool, put her arms around Joaquin's neck, and kissed him. "I'd love that," she replied. Joaquin grabbed his keys and his phone, and kissed Kerrington on the forehead.

Chapter Thirteen

"Bet, I got a new client to meet with. I'll see you at 8." Kerrington watches Joaquin walk out the door.

She sat there in a daze for a while. The ringing of her phone broke the trance. It was Lindsey. "Hey," Kerrington answered. "Uh, it's giving we need to try this again. Dry ass." Lindsey said, sarcastically. "I'm sorry, girl, my mind has been all over the place. What's up?" Kerrington replied.

"Oh, shit. Do we have another code red??" Lindsey asked, intently. "No, but you will not BELIEVE what happened to me last night!" Kerrington began to fill Lindsey in on all of the events from last night, trying not to leave out a single detail. "Friend…all that happened last night??" Lindsey asked. "Yeeesss, and my mind has been spinning since. I still don't think I've processed it all yet." "What are you gonna do about Aasir?" Lindsey asked. "What do you mean? I guess he pretty much decided that on his own." Kerrington said solemnly. Well, shit, Kerry. Can you blame him? You lucky he didn't throw that drink in your face." Lindsey said while bursting into laughter.

Kerrington sat in silence. "Awww, Kerry…you really did like him, huh?" Lindsey asked. "Probably more than I realized. Lindsey, that man made me feel invincible. He made me feel like there was NOTHING in the world I couldn't do. He was so supportive and encouraging. I've never experienced that before." Kerrington said while staring out of her kitchen window. "Kerry…do you have feelings for that man?" Lindsey asked softly. After a brief pause, a confused Kerrington answered. "Yes. I do. And don't think I actually ever realized that until now. But I guess none of that matters now.

Chapter Thirteen

What's done is done." "I know that's right! Fuck his sensitive ass!" Lindsey said as her voice escalated.

Kerrington eventually ended the call with Lindsey and started her day. Once back home, she showered and began to get ready for the evening's festivities. She put on a 3-piece crop & short set with a sheer mesh dress. She slips on some red open-toe Steve Madden heels and grabs some gold accessories. She applies her makeup and finishes it off with red matte lipstick. Kerrington gives herself one last check in the mirror before she heads out the door. "I might be a lil' overdressed, but this nigga said sexy, and I can't get much sexier than this. Shoo, sexy can't get much sexier than this. Gone, Kerrington." She says as she reaches for her small, red Marc

Chapter Thirteen

Jacobs tote. As she's leaving, she receives a text message from Joaquin. He tells her there has been a change in plans. He sends her a location and tells her to be there at 8:30.

Kerrington arrives at a building and is quickly escorted to the roof. Joaquin is standing in front of a table wearing a black blazer with a white pocket square and black slacks with a white v-neck shirt. His smile always made her weak and he smelled delicious. "Hey, you." Joaquin said, gleaming from ear to ear. "Wow, Joaquin. This is beautiful." Kerrington said as they embraced. "You're beautiful. You look amazing. But I'm glad you like it. I hope you brought your appetite with you." Joaquin says as he pulls out her chair. "Thank you, sweetie. So, you really made my favorite food? You think you sooooo slick, Joaquin Stevenson."

Kerrington said. Lamb chops, garlic potatoes, asparagus. I have a pretty decent memory." Joaquin said with a smile. "And you do. That's pretty impressive." Kerrington replied.

Kerrington and Joaquin eat, talk, and laugh for almost an hour. They reminisce about how things were when they first met and all of the things that led up to now. "He seems like a really good dude," Joaquin says as the topic shifts toward Aasir. "Yea, he was a great guy. He is a great guy." Kerrington responded. "Kerrington, I made a mistake. A mistake that I've paid for everyday since. I'm pretty sure I'm not done making mistakes, but I'm positive you not being in my life is something I'll let happen again," said Joaquin. "I miss you, Joaquin. I truly do. But at some point, I have to be smart with what I do with my heart and who I give it to. I can't just risk allowing someone to hurt me again when they already have before."

"You're right. You're 100% right. You're taking a chance on me, and I'm making a promise to you. Me breaking is the absolute last thing you'll ever have to worry about. Ever. I know this is all talk, and I know you might need some time, but check your phone," instructed Joaquin. Kerrington pulled her phone out of her tote and saw that she had received an email from Joaquin. "What's this?" she asked. "Flight details to Turk & Caicos for next weekend. As I said, you probably need some time, but, baby, I don't have any time to give you. Women like you come around once in a lifetime, KJ. Come out there with me. No pressure. No worries. Just me and you. We just vibe for a few days. Maybe this is what you need to help make up your mind.

Chapter Thirteen

You don't have to say you'll come right now. The plane leaves at 9:15 am. If you show up at the airport, I'll know all I need to know." Joaquin stated. "…and if I don't?" Kerrington asked. Joaquin paused for a second. "Then I'll know all I need to know."

Chapter Fourteen

I t's Thursday morning, and Kerrington is getting ready to do some last-minute running around before she meets up with Joaquin for their weekend getaway to Turk's & Caicos. She has an appointment at her at her new building to meet the movers who will deliver the furniture to her office. Kerrington arrives a little after 10 am and sees the movers have already started unloading the truck. Confused and worried, Kerrington gets out of her BMW and confronts one of the movers. "Ummm, excuse me. What are you guys doing? Who let you into my building?" As one mover walks by, he points

Chapter Fourteen

over his shoulder. "He did." Kerrington turns towards the door, and Aasir walks out.

"Hey…" he spoke. "Aasir, what are you doing here??" a puzzled Kerrington asked. "Well, the furniture company called and said they needed to move up the appointment. Since you still haven't officially transferred everything over into your name, when they called the realty company to see who owns the space, they got me." He explained. "Oh…well, thank you," Kerrington said. "Can we talk?" Aasir asked. "About?" Kerrington responded. "No need to be defensive. I was headed to this breakfast spot on Routh St. when they called. After that, I'm going back to Houston. Just give me a few minutes, and I'll be on my way." Aasir said. Kerrington stood in silence. "Please," Aasir added. Reluctantly, Kerrington agreed.

Chapter Fourteen

They hopped in Aasir's Escalade and drove off after the movers were done. Once they settled in and placed their orders. Aasir cut right to the chase. "Let me start by saying I apologize. After I finally calmed down that night, I realized something...I never asked if you were involved with someone. I never had a conversation with you about if there was someone else or what happened before me or anything! Although I didn't like what I heard on that call, I had no real reason to be upset because you were talking to someone from your past about the past. I reacted like a child, and for that, among other things, I sincerely apologize."

Kerrington sat there searching for the words to say. "Wow, I guess you're right. I never thought of that. I definitely understood why you were upset,

Chapter Fourteen

but you're right. I never told you about Joaquin. I think I owe you an apology as well." She replied. Aasir quickly jumped back in. "You don't. It's not your job to offer up random information to a guy you're just dating. If I wanted to know something, I should have asked. I was just too caught up in you and the pursuit of you to ask. So, keep your apology. It has no place in this discussion." Aasir said.

"Well, when you put it that way, I guess you're right." Kerrington said. So, now that we've gotten that outta the way, tell me about the guy from your past." Kerrington begins to fill Aasir in on exactly who Joaquin is and everything that transpired between the two of them. Aasir pays the tab, and they head back to the office so Kerrington can get her truck. "Well, I suppose going to take care of a child and being a family man is admirable, I suppose. But

Chapter Fourteen

got damn, that's wild." Aasir said while driving up the freeway. "Yea, I guess so. But he damn sure coulda gone about doing it a better way." Kerrington replied.

They finally pull up to the building, and Aasir walks Kerrington to her vehicle. "Come to Houston with me for the weekend. Come hang out with me." Aasir suggested. "I can't. I have plans." Kerrington advised. Aasir noticed that Kerrington wouldn't make eye contact with him as she spoke. "Wait, c'mon, Kerrington. Don't tell me you're giving this guy another chance?!" a frustrated Aasir said. "Uh, uh, don't do that. Don't try to chastise me for giving him something you want!" Kerrington fired back. "You're giving a man who chose someone else another chance and didn't even have the common decency to tell you why. I've chosen you from DAY ONE because it's been you and ONLY you from day one. He and I are not the same."

"Wow, not you dirty mackin' Joaquin," Kerrington said sarcastically. "Is it dirty mackin', or is it the truth? I don't know that man, nor do I care to know him. I know you thought I was trying to buy you when we first met. I could tell how hesitant you were to let your guard down with me, but over time you saw what was real. You saw a man that was pouring into you with no ulterior motive. You wanna know why? Because I see something in you that he doesn't. I know your self-worth. And if he did, if he truly knew your self-worth and respected it, he wouldn't have left you the way he did. I've known the value of your self-worth from the moment I laid eyes on you. And the funny thing is, if someone truly respects your self-worth, that respect will prevent them from compromising it. I walked out of that restaurant because I didn't think you respected mine. I was wrong. Ask yourself this: I'll choose you a hundred times out of a hundred. Regardless of the situation. Will he?"

The night turned into morning, and Kerrington awoke and got herself together so she could meet Joaquin at the airport. As she walked through the sliding doors, she saw Joaquin standing there, smiling. "Thank you for coming! I can't tell you how happy I am that you decided to come." Joaquin said as he hugged Kerrington. "Babe, where are your bags? You already checked 'em in?" he asked. "No," Kerrington replied. "No? Why not?? Are they still in the car? I can go get 'em. Gimme your keys." Joaquin said as he held out his hand.

"Joaquin, I didn't bring any bags with me. I'm not going." Joaquin stood there. Stunned. "I just came to tell you in person."

"But, why?" Joaquin asked as he looked at her dejectedly. "I can't do this, Joaquin. I can't. Not showing up here and telling you face-to-face would have been a coward's way out. I talked to Aasir last night..." Joaquin quickly cut Kerrington off. "Aasir?? Fuck Aasir!! You choosing him over me??" Joaquin yelled. "No, Joaquin! I'm choosing ME over YOU!! I'm choosing someone who will choose me every single time!! No matter the situation! I told you I have to be careful with who I give my heart to. I don't expect you to understand, and it's not my job to make you understand."

Chapter Fourteen

Kerrington turned around and walked away. She began to walk a bit faster as the tears began to well up in her eyes. Joaquin stood at the end of the terminal. Confused. Angry. Hurt. Devastated. He dug into his right pocket, pulled out a small velvet box, and opened it. He stared at the engagement ring he was set to propose with on the trip. He closed the box, put it back in his pocket, and watched Kerrington walk away until he could no longer see her. Joaquin couldn't help but feel as if he had just watched his future turn into his past.

Is "love" enough? Who really knows? I'm sure for some people it is, but I'm just as sure for some people, it isn't. For Kerrington, it wasn't. She loves Joaquin with every fiber in her bones. Through and through. But at this place in her life, she desires someone to love her just as much as she loves herself. So, in the end she chose someone who did. She chose herself.

Peace, love, and happiness starts with you. And in order to receive it properly, you must love yourself first, and provide **yourself** with peace and happiness. Once you obtain that level self- love and serenity, you won't allow anyone to give you anything less than what you are already giving yourself.

Both Joaquin and Aasir regretted how they handled things with Kerrington, and they both were sincerely sorry for the mistakes they made. There's nothing wrong with apologizing and admitting your faults, but that doesn't mean the person on the other end has to accept it. Apologies don't fix everything because everything can't be fixed with an apology.

In the end, you can debate who you believe would have been the better suitor for Kerrington, but what isn't debatable is that she walked out of that airport confident and with no regrets…

Or did she?

Make sure you scan the QR code

to download the Jonesing

Soundtrack on Apple Music and

Spotify!!

Apple 

Spotify

www.ingramcontent.com/pod-product-compliance
Lightning Source LLC
Chambersburg PA
CBHW061246120726
48001CB00001B/178